Orr's Truisms

Bert K. Orr

ISBN - 1440491887
EAN-13 - 9781440491887.

Cover and interior design by TFS

Forward

A 'Truism' is a statement, the truth of which is obvious or well known.

I don't know when I started collecting 'truisms' or exactly why. I have always been fascinated by inspirational thoughts and a voracious reader, so I guess it just happened.

As I wrote them down and the collection started to grow, I then needed to do something with all of these random thoughts.

Several years ago I started finding willing volunteers to type up five or six sheets at a time, then I would start giving them out to friends or people that I encountered who were soon to become friends. This grew into a list of eighty-plus 'friends' all over the country and who are on my quarterly mailing list.

Some just enjoy the smiles, some can't wait for new material for speeches and newsletters, but for me it's a way to stay connected with people I have encountered over my ninety years here on planet earth. After I do a mailing, I get phone calls and notes from all over the country. In these days of hurry and rush it's a wonderful thing.

Bert K. Orr

Acknowledgment:

A heart filled "thank you" to Chuck and Tom Shubnell – brothers and good friends who suggested and compiled this book. Also, thanks to all that went before, there is 'no such thing as an original thought' and this book is a collection of a multitude of funny, wonderful, and inspirational thoughts that I have collected over many decades, whose authors go unnamed.

Have a real happy day today! Enjoy it because you got up this morning.

Table of Contents

Time and Ageing

Time and Ageing

We do not remember days - we remember moments.

With every rising of the sun, think of life as just begun.

If only we could think twice and still be in the conversation.

Be interested in the future, because you're going to spend the rest of your life there.

Everyday is an opportunity to do something you've never done before.

Lose an hour in the morning and you will be all day hunting it.

One of the greatest enemies we can ever face is the illusion that there will be more time tomorrow than today.

We too soon get old, and too late get smart.

You can't build a reputation on what you are going to do.

The trouble with time is that you don't learn to make the most of it until most of it is gone.

Dreams come true for those who don't oversleep.

A true procrastinator is one who puts off until tomorrow what has already been put off until today.

A timely present for an always tardy person is an alarm clock.

How long a minute is depends on which side of the bathroom door you're on.

For every minute of action, there should be an hour of thought.

Sixty seconds of being happy are lost every minute you are mad.

Half our life is spent trying to find something to do with the time we have rushed through life trying to save.

Nothing in the world arouses more false hopes than the first four hours of a day.

An optimist is a person who leaves the dishes because he thinks he will feel more like doing them in the morning.

When the sun goes down let it take the day's troubles with it.

When the time of need arises, the time for planning has passed.

Nature gives you the face you have at 20. It is up to you to merit the face you have at 50.

Regret demands payment of your time, but renders you no service.

How long a minute takes is dependent on which side of the bathroom door you're on.

Procrastination is the art of keeping up with yesterday.

You are only young once, but you can stay immature indefinitely.

The sunrise never finds us where the sunset left us.

People spend so much time fretting about what they did yesterday and dreading what might happen tomorrow, they miss out on all of their todays.

Our golden age is never the present age.

Yesterday is history. Tomorrow is a mystery. Today is a gift. That's why it's called: The Present.

How old would you be if you didn't know how old you are?

You may not be able to turn back the clock, but you can always wind it up again.

There is no such thing in anyone's life as an unimportant day.

There is no royal road to anything. One thing at a time, and all things in succession. That which grows slowly endures.

Today is the tomorrow you worried about yesterday.

True maturity consists in mellowing with the years and growing old gratefully.

Time and Ageing

Lost time is never found again.

An old belief is like an old shoe. We so value its comfort that we fail to notice the hole in it.

Our worst misfortunes never happen, and most, miseries lie in anticipation.

There is no sadder sight than a young pessimist, except and old optimist.

Old age is when you buy a birthday cake and the baker throws in a smoke alarm for free.

You've been around for quite some time if you remember when the first person an accident victim asked for was a doctor, not a lawyer.

Take rest; a field that has rested gives a bountiful crop.

The young have aspirations that never come to pass. The old have reminiscences of what never happened.

Everything cometh to he who waiteth, as long as he who waiteth works like hell while he waiteth.

Why is there no expiration date on sour cream?

The future belongs to those who believe in the beauty of their dreams.

We must strive to die young at a very old age.

If you are patient in one moment of anger, you will escape a hundred days of sorrow.

You are mature when you know what is foolhardy and what is courage.

I don't like Fridays—they're to close to Mondays.

Ever notice how we get older so much faster than we grow up?

Worry pulls tomorrow's cloud over today's sunshine.

Old age should be regarded as a reward for a lifetime of hard work, but it can only be a punishment if one insists on doing the same things one has always done, measuring present achievements by past ones and inevitably falling short.

Tradition is what once was a bright new idea.

It's not too late to run away and join the circus.

The only limits to our realization of tomorrow will be our doubts of today.

Procrastination is a habit that most of us are going to break tomorrow.

In youth we learn, in old age we understand.

One time we should procrastinate is when we think we should get even with somebody.

Gossip travels with the speed of delight.

It's nice to know that no matter how many birthdays you have, you're never as old as your children think you are.

By the time we reach 50, the face we have is the one we deserve.

Every year it seems to take less time to *fly* across the ocean and longer to drive to work.

Everything is relative. Years ago, women thought that the washboard was a great technological advancement compared to pounding clothes on a rock.

Three enemies of personal peace:
1. Regret over yesterday's mistakes;
2. Anxiety over tomorrow's problems;
3. Ingratitude for today's blessings.

Retirees think each week has six Saturdays, then Sunday. Chuck thinks there are seven Saturdays.

If pleasures are greatest in anticipation, just remember that this is also true of trouble.

Every passing day is one that is gone forever, make sure it is one in which you have done something for others, especially those who cannot do for themselves.

We cannot alter the past, but we can be alert for the future.

When we consider when to begin, it becomes too late.

The trouble with traveling in the fast lane is that you get to the other end in an awful hurry.

Time and Ageing

Lost, somewhere between sunrise and sunset, 60 golden minutes, each set with 60 diamond seconds. No reward is offered, for they are gone forever.

It's not too difficult to acquire the habit of punctuality; it's just a matter of time.

The man who is a pessimist before 48 knows too much; if he is an optimist after it, he knows too little.

The best preparation for tomorrow is doing your best today.

One trouble with most of us is that we spend too much of our present planning how to spend our future.

The time to mind somebody else's business is when he doesn't.

If pleasures are greatest in anticipation, just remember that is also true of troubles.

Procrastination is opportunity's natural assassin.

I have always been in the right place at the right time. Of course, I steered myself there.

Don't think everyone is a Sunday driver. It might be a Friday driver still looking for a place to park.

Age is important only in dead fish and good wine.

Ever notice that as you get older the days get longer but the years shorter?

At your 25th class reunion, you wear a name tag so your classmates can remember who you are. At your 50th reunion, you wear one so you can remember who you are.

No man is to be pitied except the one whose future lies behind.

It takes retirement to reveal the joy of work.

Remember senior citizens, it's all relative, so be of good cheer. To a five-year old, a ten-year old is a senior citizen.

Life is too short to waste time complaining about how short it is.

Nothing makes you realize how precious time is till you pay a parking garage.

At my age, it's always something I have to live with or something I have to live without.

Do not put off until tomorrow what you can do today - tomorrow there may he a law against it.

Time spent trying to get even is better used trying to get ahead.

Old age is when your favorite theme park is slumberland.

Some men defy old age. They still believe that they as good as they never were.

When pointing to another's past, remember it's his history - not his destiny.

Being an accomplished worrier makes today's problems seem trivial compared to what you imagine will go wrong tomorrow.

The only thing I know about the speed of light is that it gets here much too early in the morning.

Sometimes I wonder why people knock themselves out to always be on time. Likely as not, there is no one present to appreciate it.

The trouble with being young is that you're not old enough to enjoy it.

Spend each day as if it was your last and you'll be broke by sunset.

It takes time to grow old, and I've never had any.

If the thought of getting older makes you blue think of this: a lot of people never do.

To worry about your age is silly, Every time you're a year older so is everyone else.

Nothing really makes the younger generation seem so bad as having lost your membership in it.

Anger is the only thing to put off until tomorrow.

Spring is nature's way of saying "Let's Party!"

You're getting old when you stoop to tie your shoes and wonder what else you can do while you're down there.

Time and Ageing

Tomorrow is a dream romance. Today is a lover to enjoy.

Everyone wants to live long, but no one wants to grow old.

Perhaps the secret of life is to run out of years before we run out of dreams.

It's not the number of years that makes you old, but the idea that you are getting old.

Growing older isn't upsetting, being perceived as old is.

Just remember, once you're over the hill you begin to pick up speed.

Age is not important unless you're a cheese.

Every day is a gift, so don't rap it.

A man doesn't just grow old. He becomes old by not growing.

The only limit to our realization of tomorrow will be our doubts of today.

The present is colored by the past but we can choose the colors of the future.

Live today as though you were going to die tomorrow and have to answer for it.

Retirement is when you reach an age when you still have a first-class mind, but your body is going tourist.

There is no better way to fight old age than by refusing to act the part.

You're not too old if you prefer dates to prunes.

If you live by the calendar, your days are numbered.

You are never too old to learn and never too young to know it all.

Mondays are a hard way to spend one seventh of your life.

You can discover more about a person in an hour of play than in a year of conversation.

The secret of staying young is to live honestly, eat slowly, and lie about your age.

Try to make at least one person smile today.

It is well to be up before daybreak, for such habits contribute to health, wealth and wisdom.

When you're young, try to be realistic; as you get older, become idealistic. You'll live longer.

Cherish all your happy moments they make a fine cushion for old age.

Every age is modern to those who are living it.

Peace is seeing a sunset and knowing who to thank.

When you're young, try to be realistic; as you get older, become idealistic you'll live longer.

If you learn something new every day, the days are not wasted.

The going gets easier when you are over the hill.

The bad news is that time flies, the good news is that you're the pilot.

Its not that age brings childhood back again, age merely shows what children we remain.

Spring is when you feel like whistling even with a shoe full of slush.

Do you resent growing old? Many are denied the privilege.

A person lost in his work has probably found his future.

A guest sees more in an hour than a host sees in a year.

Youth looks ahead, old age looks back and middle age looks tired.

You know you're aging if you get lost strolling down Memory Lane.

Impatience is waiting in a hurry.

To live long, live slowly.

The chief worries of life arise from the foolish habit of looking before and after.

You can't get much done by starting tomorrow.

Time and Ageing

You can't back the clock up, but you can wind it up again.

It's hard to judge the age of a person whose spirit has remained young.

To me, old age is always 15 years older than I am.

Sunset in one land is sunrise in another.

Don't let the future scare you, its as uncertain as you are.

A sign in a small town has to be admired for its cynical honesty "Antique tables made daily."

It's only when the tide goes out that you learn who's been swimming naked.

You can spend it any way you wish, but you can spend it only once.

Plant a tree to live in the faraway future.

May is nature's way of apologizing for February.

At my age I've seen it all, I've heard it all, I've done it all, but I just can't remember it all.

Age is not important, unless you are cheese.

We can improve our tomorrows with a better understanding of our yesterdays.

Be not afraid of moving slowly: be afraid of standing still.

In summer, the song sings itself.

"Do you know when you're getting old?" my friend asked. "I give up," I said.

Each day comes bearing gifts - it's up to you to untie the ribbons.

Many people die at twenty-five and aren't buried until they are seventy-five.

You're only young once, but you can be immature all your life.

Middle age is when your age starts to show around your middle.

He decided to live forever or die in the attempt.

Sex after ninety is like trying to shoot pool with a rope.

Crossing the street in New York keeps old people young - if they make it.

The past always looks better than it was because it isn't here.

Getting old is a fascinating thing. The older you get, the older you want to get.

When you win, you're an old pro, when you lose you're an old man.

You can take no credit for beauty at 16, but if you are beautiful at 60, it will be your soul's own doing.

The day the Lord created hope was probably the same day he created spring.

We are of a generation that went from outdoor plumbing to indoor swimming in one generation.

Get a good night's sleep; things will look better in the morning.

It's easy enough to be pleasant when life goes by like a song, but the man worthwhile is the man who can smile after everything else goes wrong.

There's a first time for everything.

I have more time than money, and sharing time with others is what life is all about.

It takes one hand to do dishes today, tomorrow it will take two.

If you have time to do it over, you have time to do it right.

Nobody will know how long it took you to do this; all they'll know is what it looks like when you're done.

No matter how busy you are, you owe yourself at least enough time out of each day to read.

Those who make the worst use of their time are the first to complain of its brevity.

Do nothing hastily but catching of fleas.

To perfect the character; live each day as if the last.

Time and Ageing

Each day of life is spent, and leaves the balance smaller.

Don't worry about the other fellow's life or you'll be robbing yourself of some of your own.

Life is short; the present should be turned to profit with reasonableness and right.

To focus on the future helps fling away the vagaries of the past.

Time and tide wait for no man.

The only thing that doesn't slow down as you get older is the rate at which everything slows down!

Make it a point to do something every day that you don't want to do. This is the golden rule for acquiring the habit of doing your duty without pain.

Don't part with your illusions. When they are gone you may still exist, but you have ceased to live.

Each person is born to one possession which out values all his others - his last breath.

It is never too late to give up our prejudices.

One of the problems with living for the moment is that a moment doesn't last very long.

The key to success is setting aside eight hours a day for work and eight hours for sleep, and making sure they're not the same hours.

Don't borrow trouble from tomorrow, tomorrow will take care of itself.

Let's not cross that bridge until we come to it.

Experience enables you to recognize a mistake when you make it again.

To choose time is to save time.

Growing old is only a state of mind brought on by gray hair, false teeth, wrinkles, a big belly, shortness of breath and being constantly totally pooped.

You cannot do a kindness too soon, for you never know how soon it will be too late.

Growing old is inevitable...growing up is optional.

A man who dares to waste one hour of time has not discovered the value of life.

Young at heart. . . slightly older in other places.

Worrying does not empty tomorrow of its troubles, it empties today of its strength.

Times flies, but you are the navigator.

A wise man learns from the mistakes of others. Nobody lives long enough to make them all himself.

Nothing keeps a heart feeling younger than looking at the world through the eyes of a child.

Old age is always ten years older than you are.

You know you are getting old when you stoop to tie your shoelaces and wonder what else you can do as long as you are already down there.

Don't do everything today. Save some mistakes for tomorrow.

Prayer is too often like a lamp that isn't used until it starts to get dark.

If you wait too long to get your life on the right track, you just may find out that the train has already left.

Growing older isn't upsetting, being perceived as old is.

Few things have a shorter life than a clean garage.

When we're young we want to change the world: When we're old we want to change the young.

It takes time to grow old and I have never had any.

One of the advantages of being young is that you don't let common sense get in the way of doing things that everybody knows are impossible.

We will never enter much in our journal of accomplishment if we always wait for the right time to do anything.

If you want to leave footprints in the sand of time, don't drag your feet.

Time and Ageing

Many people worry a lot today about tomorrow, because they didn't worry a little yesterday about today.

Yesterday's sin is today's lifestyle.

The past gives us experience and memories; the present gives us challenges and opportunities; the future gives us vision and hope.

The years teach much which the days never know.

Nothing ages a fellow faster than trying to prove he's still as young as ever.

A weatherman is a guy who tells you today what is going to happen tomorrow and then the next day explains why it didn't.

Look at the bright side: No matter how old you are – you are younger than you will ever be again.

Enthusiasm is what enables some folks to die of old age without ever having seemed old.

No one is ever as old as he hopes to be.

The real secret of staying young is being to busy to think about it.

Friendship and Kindness

Friendship and Kindness

The law sent us our relatives, but thank God, we can choose our friends ourselves.

A friend is long sought, hardly found, and with difficulty kept.

We need old friends to help us grow old and new friends to help us stay young.

Treat your family like friends and your friends like family.

Offering advice may be noble and grand, but it's not the same as a helping hand.

If all my friends jumped off a cliff I wouldn't jump with them. I would be at the bottom to catch them.

Kindness is the golden chain by which society is bound together.

Love always finds a warm home in the heart of a friend.

It's nice to how that when you help someone up a hill, you're a little nearer the top yourself.

The only rose without a thorn is friendship.

Any relationship where you put yourself first won't last.

Gossip can turn friends into enemies; forgiveness can change enemies into friends.

Friendship is a treasury; you cannot take from it more than you put into it.

Praise does wonders for the sense of hearing.

You cannot live a perfect day without doing something for someone who will never be able to repay you.

Friendship is not how you forget, but how you forgive.

A man never discloses his own character so clearly as when he describes another's.

Kindness is the oil that takes the friction out of life.

There is a destiny that makes us brothers. No one goes his way alone; all that we send into the hearts of others comes back into our own.

The deepest principle of human nature is the craving to be appreciated.

The wrong way to pick your friends is to pieces.

Too many people insult friends and flatter strangers.

Some people make the world more special just by being in it.

A true friend is one who notices when you lose a pound, but not when you gain ten.

It is wise to observe our own faults with a magnifying glass; the faults of others, with a telescope.

The best thing to do behind a friend's back is pat it.

Sweep first before your own door, before you sweep the doorsteps of neighbors.

Friendship is not how you listen, but how you understand.

No one can give you inner strength, but sometimes they can help you find it.

Find peace within, and your world will look fresh and new, see good in others, and they soon see good in you.

When you help a man in trouble you can be sure of one thing. He won't forget you the next time he's in trouble.

To a shut-in a friendly telephone call is like a beautiful gift.

It's what the guests say as they pull out of the driveway that really counts.

Don't tell your friends their social faults; they will cure the fault and never forgive you.

Treat people as if they were what they ought to be and you help them become what they are capable of becoming.

What can you give people who 'have everything'? Give them sympathy most of them are in need of it.

Friendship and Kindness

A true test of character is being put on a pedestal and not looking down on those who put you there.

Flattery is like alcohol: If it makes you want more, you've had to much.

Most of us admire the person who dares to be different - unless it is us he's different from.

Telling folks where to get off is not the best way to get on.

The best way to forget your own problems is to help someone else solve theirs.

A good exercise for the heart is to bend down and help another up.

Many people will walk in and out of your life, but only true friends will leave footprints in your heart.

Friendship is forgetting what one gives and remembering what one receives.

A smile is a curve that can straighten out a lot of things.

Friendship is not how you see, but how you feel.

If you wait too long for your ship to come in, it just may dock at another port.

True friends are those that really know you but love you anyway.

Treasure is not always a friend, but a friend is always a treasure.

Carry out a random act of kindness—safe in the knowledge that one day someone might do the same for you.

If we are to bury the hatchet, we bury the handle as well.

You'll always be my best friend, you know too much.

When a friend deals with a friend, let the bargain be clear and well penned, that they may continue friends to the end.

If you would keep your secret from an enemy, tell it not to a friend.

A brother may not he a friend, but a friend will always he a brother.

A best friend is a sister that destiny forgot to give you.

Be kind, every person you meet is fighting a hard battle.

A boo is a lot louder than a cheer.

Correction does much, but encouragement does more.

Getting people to like you is simply the other side of liking other people.

You can't shake hands with a clenched fist.

The meanest, most contemptible kind of praise is that which first speaks well of a man, and then qualifies it with a "but."

If you can't apologize, you'd better be good at making new friends.

An enemy is an injured friend.

My palms used to get sweaty when I thought a girl would say 'No' now they get sweaty when I think she'll say 'Yes'.

You will never get a dizzy feeling by doing too many good turns.

Feelings are everywhere—be gentle.

A real friend is one who will continue to talk to you over the back fence even though he knows he's missing his television program.

Good companions are folks who pretend to enjoy being bored.

If you want friends, you must learn to speak their language.

Kindness is a language the deaf can hear and the dumb can understand.

Real friends don't ask you for money unless you owe it to them.

Flattery does little harm, and criticism little good.

There is nothing as good as goodwill. It creates love, cements relationships, and restores our faith in humanity.

Courtesy is the shortest distance between two people.

Many people prefer to believe the best of everybody—it saves trouble.

If you offer somebody a helping hand, you should not put a condition in it.

Be smarter than other people, just don't tell them so.

Good manners sometimes means simply putting up with other peoples bad manners.

Remember that the most valuable antiques are dear old friends.

The more arguments you win, the fewer friends, you'll have.

Send the flowers when the man gets well, instead of when he doesn't.

See others through the lenses of love; judge then through the filters of kindness.

Others want us to look at them; not through them; to talk with them not about them.

The only people you should ever want to get "even" with are those who have helped you.

Take a tip from the tombstones - never do anything but praise a man when he's down.

Nothing brightens up the other fellow's conversation like an unexpected compliment from him about you.

I have a friend who's not in need, that's what I call a friend.

Good friends are the diplomas of the school of life.

The really special person is the one who treats all others as though they were.

He receives most favors who knows how to return them.

Promises may get you friends but it is performance that keeps them.

A sandwich with a friend is usually better than a steak by yourself.

If you're looking for friends, find those who need you.

Real friendship is shown in times of trouble; prosperity is full of friends.

He who tries to buy friendship knows nothing about the product.

Close your eyes to the faults of others and watch the doors of friendship swing wide open.

Pick your friends, but not to pieces.

The way to have friends is to be willing to lose some arguments.

It's always good to lend a sympathetic ear, but sometimes hard to get it back.

Only the person who has faith in himself is able to be faithful to others.

If you don't want to undo a friendship, don't try to outdo a friend.

If you treat everybody courteously, it will surprise you how courteous they all become.

If you want to be well liked, never lie about yourself and be careful about telling the truth about others.

Grief yearns for compassion, not advice.

Despite your height, you grow six inches when somebody expresses confidence in you.

You can make more friends in two months by becoming interested in other people than you can in two years by trying to get other people interested in you.

If you're not willing to be a friend to someone who doesn't entirely suit you, you'll never have many friends.

Friends are those rare people who ask how we are and then wait to hear the answer.

A good test of willpower is to meet a friend with a black eye and not ask any questions.

Kindness is the golden chain by which society is bound together.

The proper duty of a friend is to side with you when you are in the wrong. Nearly anybody will side with you when you are in the right.

Nobody has ever come up with a good substitute for friendship.

One's worst enemy is the one disguised as a friend.

Most people enjoy the inferiority of their best friends.

A real friend never gets in your way unless you happen to be on your way down.

A true friend is someone who is there for you when he would rather be somewhere else.

You can knock the chip off another person's shoulder simply by patting him on the back.

Only the person who has faith in himself is able to be faithful to others.

The best mirror is often a good friend.

A good friend will come and bail you out of jail, but, a true friend will be sitting next to you saying, "Wow, that was fun!"

True friendship is like sound health; the value of it is seldom known until it be lost.

Good friends are good for your health.

Flattery is like chewing gum. Enjoy it but don't swallow it.

Our duty is not to see through one another, but to see one another through.

It's better to be looked over than to be overlooked.

What is done for another is done for oneself.

Write a letter in order to get one.

I felt it shelter to speak to you.

The most I can do for my friend is simply to be his friend.

Friendship flourishes at the fountain of forgiveness.

Friends are made by many acts - and lost by only one.

The better part of one's life consists of his friendships.

Be slow in choosing a friend, slower in changing.

The best preservative to keep the mind in health is the faithful admonition of a friend.

Friendship improves happiness, and abates misery, by doubling our joy, and dividing our grief.

Don't ever get so rich that you can afford to lose a friend.

Hold a true friend with both hands.

One kindness can warm three winter months.

Giving is living, if you stop wanting to give there's nothing more to live for.

Friendship is love—with understanding.

Live so your friends can defend you, but never have to.

No small act of kindness is ever wasted.

To understand people you must understand their memories.

Trying to dim someone else's light doesn't make yours shine any brighter.

When a best friend is told you're having an affair they ask, "Is it catered?"

The only way to have a friend is to be one.

I have yet to be bored by someone paying me a compliment.

The light of friendship is like the light of phosphorous, seen when all around is dark.

Words in haste do friendships waste.

Some people come into our lives and leave footprints on our hearts. And we are never, ever the same.

People are like stained-glass windows; they sparkle and shine when the sun is out, but when the darkness sets in, their true beauty is revealed only if there is a light within.

Of all the things which wisdom provides to make life entirely happy, the greatest is the possession of friendship.

From quiet homes and first beginning, out to the undiscovered ends, there's nothing worth the wear of winning, but laughter and the love of friends.

Friendship and Kindness

A word from a friend is doubly enjoyable in dark days.

No man can be happy without a friend, nor be sure of his friend until he is unhappy.

Our lives are filled with simple joys and blessings without end. And one of the greatest joys in life is to have a friend.

Friendship is the shadow of the evening, which strengthens with the setting of the sun of life.

He alone has lost the art to live who cannot win new friends.

Friendships are fragile things, and require as much care in handling as any other fragile and precious thing.

Life has no blessing like a prudent friend.

The loss of a friend is like that of a limb; time may heal the anguish of the wound, but the loss cannot be repaired.

A friend that you have to buy won't be worth what you pay for him, no matter what that may be.

Two persons cannot long be friends if they cannot forgive each other's little failings.

Friends feed each other, and not just bread and soup. Friends feed each other's spirits and dreams and hopes; they feed each other with the things a soul needs to live.

Life is to be fortified by many friendships. To love and be loved is the greatest happiness of existence.

Kind words can never die.

Kindness is to do and say, the kindest things in the kindest way.

Never feel hatred for another person. You can hate what they do or what they say, but never say, "I hate you."

Be kind and gentle to those who are old, for kindness is dearer and better than gold.

Kill them with kindness.

If an elderly person drops something, kindly pick it up for them.

To have a friend, you must be one.

Make new friends, but keep the old, One is silver and the other gold.

The best thing to do behind one's back is pat it.

If you're worried about someone talking about you behind your back, don't worry, they're just leaving someone else alone,

There is so much good in the worst of us, and so much bad in the best of us, that it little behooves any of us-to talk about the rest of us.

Never believe anything bad that you hear of anyone, and only half of what you see, because all you see is not what it appears to be.

Never say something about someone you wouldn't say to their face.

When you feel the urge to repeat some gossip, bite your tongue.

If you use your friends like a light switch, beware, you may burn out the bulb.

Birds of a feather flock together.

It is good and pleasant when people dwell in unity.

Those who have successful friendships allow their loved ones room. Rather than possessing their friends, they try to help them expand and grow and become free.

The best friend does not worry about how many friends to count, but rather that he or she can be a friend to be counted on.

If we build more windows and fewer walls, we will have more friends.

God gives us our relatives, but we choose our friends.

Tell me who you associate with, and I'll tell you who you are.

Said about making a difficult decision - People who mind don't matter, and people who matter won't mind.

Never criticize someone's words or deeds until you've walked in their shoes.

Just wash your own windows and your neighbor's house won't look half as dirty.

Friendship and Kindness

Be sure to sweep in front of your own doorstep.

Always remember - you are just as good as anyone, but not one bit better.

People do the very best they know how at the time they are doing it.

There is a little good in everyone.

Don't judge a book by its cover.

If you aren't good at entertaining yourself, you aren't good at entertaining anyone else.

Dig a hole for your neighbor and you'll fall into it yourself.

Friends bring out the beautiful things in each other that no one else looks hard enough to find.

Gratitude gives as much pleasure to the giver as to the recipient.

Goodwill is desiring good, planning for good, and doing good.

All that falls to the benefit of the individual is a benefit to the whole, or what does not benefit the hive is of no benefit to the bee.

Make your friends your teachers and mingle the pleasures of conversation with the advantages of instruction.

There is less harm to be suffered in being mad among madmen than in being sane all by oneself.

We may take Fancy for a companion, but must follow Reason as our guide.

It takes your enemy and your friend, working together, to hurt you to the heart; the one to slander you and the other to get the news to you.

If you pray for another, you will be helped yourself.

A friend is the thermometer by which we may judge the temperature of our fortune.

A friend is one who is here today and here tomorrow.

A friend is someone with whom you can be silent.

Friendship is a treasury: You cannot take from it more than you put into it.

Friendship is the only cement that will hold the world together.

Friendship is expecting a great deal from one another but never asking for it.

A man or a woman is as good as their word.

You don't live in a world all alone. Your brothers are here, too.

Have therefore first zeal to thyself, and then mayest thou have zeal to thy neighbor.

He who helps a child helps humanity with an immediateness which no other help given to human creature in any other stage of human life can possibly give again.

Man becomes great exactly in the degree in which he works for the welfare of his fellow men.

The only gift is a portion of thyself.

If a man be gracious and courteous to strangers, it shows he is a citizen of the world, and that his heart is no island cut off from other lands, but a continent that joins them.

The greatest pleasure I know is to do a good action by stealth, and to have it found out by accident.

After all there is but one race - humanity.

Blessed are those who can give without remembering, and take without forgetting.

Your neighbor is the man who needs you.

What do we live for, if it is not to make life less difficult for each other?

Any kindness I can show, or any good thing I can do, let me do it now; let me not defer it or neglect it, for I shall not pass this way again.

The human contribution is the essential ingredient. It is only in the giving of oneself to others that we truly live.

A person is a person because he recognizes others as persons. When you are good to others, you are best to yourself.

Don't walk in front of me, I may not follow. Don't walk behind me, I may not lead. Walk beside me and just be my friend.

A friend understands what you are trying to say, even when your thoughts aren't fitting into words.

Yes, we must ever be friends; and of all who offer you friendship, let me be the first, the truest, the nearest and dearest.

In friendship your heart is like a bell struck every time your friend is in trouble.

The smallest good deed is better than the greatest good intention.

There's never a dull moment when I'm out with Eddie. It lasts the whole evening.

You are meeting a friend when you don't worry about the impression you're making.

One of the quickest ways to meet new people is to pick up the wrong ball on a golf course.

If your heart rules your head, you'll lack money. If your head rules your heart, you'll lack friends.

The smallest kindness may be remembered forever.

True friends are those rare people who ask how you are - and then wait to hear the answer.

Friendship is like money, easier made than kept.

Never interrupt when you are being flattered.

There are too many people who think tenderness and weakness are the same thing.

Feeling gratitude and not expressing it is like wrapping a present and not giving it.

Do something every day to make other people happy, even if it's only to leave them alone.

A compliment is of no value until you give it to somebody.

When it comes to doing things for others, some people will stop at nothing.

It's amazing how quickly snobs turn into nice people when they remember your first name.

Trouble with the world is that we care more about keeping up with the Jones more than we care about the Jones.

There is less pain in biting your tongue than in losing a friendship.

Listening is one of the most helpful things you can do for most persons.

When a person grows to like himself, he becomes more tolerant of others.

We ought to treat strangers as if we expected to see them again.

To believe all men honest would be folly. To believe no man is honest is something worse.

Better the bite of a friend than the kiss of an enemy.

Nothing brings people together more quickly than shared grief or shared greed.

The nicest thing you can give a person is something to feel important about.

Willingness to make amends has much to do with keeping friends.

Friends won by favors are easily lost to others willing to do more for them.

If it were not for our fears there would not be so many strangers.

There is no accomplishment so easy to acquire as politeness, and none more profitable.

The people we remember after they are gone are the people who remembered us while they were alive.

Why be hard on yourself when your friends are so willing to do it for you?

Solitude teaches us how much we need others, yet being with others too much teaches us how much we also need solitude.

Express approval, but send criticism by slow freight.

Some folks say what they think, others have friends.

He will never have a true friend who is afraid of making enemies.

To live and let live is good. To live and help live is better.

You can't act like a skunk without someone getting wind of it.

Believe the best rather than the worst.

People hate a way of living up or down to your opinion of them.

Lips function better in kissing than in criticizing.

Friends who send postcards with the message, "WISH YOU WERE HERE," are saying, "LOOK WHERE I AM!"

One can give another no greater gift than hope.

A major form of charity is giving someone the benefit of the doubt.

No one will remain sad who finds a way to cheer a depressed friend.

If you set out to find fault, you'll not likely find perfection.

Friendliness is insulation against another's anger.

If the faults we see in others were not so much like our own, we would not recognize them so easily.

Instead of loving your enemies, why not treat your friends a little better?

If you can't be happy for another's success, you don't deserve your own.

The most welcome person is the one who knows when to go.

Gentleness never closes a door nor finds one it cannot open.

True test of friendship is if you'd do more for him than he can do for you.

A gentle answer quiets anger, but a harsh one stirs it up.

Kind acts are more effective than sermons and make you feel much better.

If you want an accounting of your worth, count your friends.

True friendship is like sound health; the value of it is seldom known until it is lost.

If you tell the truth, you don't have to remember anything.

If I take care of my character, my reputation will take of itself.

A man who pays an ounce of principal for a pound of popularity gets badly cheated.

Resentment hurts only those who harbor it.

Always give people more than they expect to get.

Secrets are things we give to others to keep for us.

Gossip is the art of saying nothing in a way that leaves nothing unsaid.

Real friends are those who see heart to heart when they don't see eye to eye.

The easiest way to feel good is to do good.

When it comes to sincerity, style is everything.

You will be considered good at small talk if you just listen.

The deepest feeling always shows itself in silence.

A friend is a present you give yourself.

Never ask a relative for a favor nor a friend for a loan.

Anyone who will gossip to you about others will gossip to others about you.

The best thing about Alzheimer's disease is you get to meet new people every day.

You cannot do a kindness too soon, for you never know how soon it will be too late.

A person who is nice to you, but rude to a waiter, is not a nice person.

We can't help everyone, but everyone can help someone.

Do something bad and regret it; do something good and forget it.

Kindness is the golden chain by which society is bound together.

There ain't no surer way to find out whether you like people or hate them than to travel with them.

Friendship and Kindness

Tact is the art of making guests feel at home when that's really where you wish they were.

Kind words can be short and easy to speak, but their echoes are truly endless.

The most important thing in communication is to hear what isn't being said.

A real friend is one who walks in when the rest of the world walks out.

We never get dizzy from doing good turns.

Say what you mean, mean what you say, and do not be mean when you say it.

Revenge, a dish best served cold.

People who want to share their religious views with you almost never want you to share yours with them.

Friends are folks who have faults you pretend not to notice.

The only rose without a thorn is friendship.

One friend in a lifetime is much, two are many, and three are hardly possible.

Food and Diet

Food and Diet

Dieting can be summed up in one, word - snackrifice.

I think I see your problem. You own a hundred cookbooks and one sex manual.

Chocolate makes my clothes shrink.

Families are like fudge, mostly sweet with a few nuts.

You are what you eat, as a rule of thumb: The more you eat, the more you become.

What was the best thing before sliced bread?

The food that never goes up in price is food for thought.

Only dull people are brilliant at breakfast.

Food is always an important part of a balanced diet.

On average 100 people choke to death on ballpoint pens every year.

People who "pan" dieting develop a "pot".

It would be a lot easier to lose weight and keep it off if the replacement parts weren't so easily available in the refrigerator.

I've never met a carbohydrate that I didn't like!

Good intentions, like choice fruit, are perishable and difficult to keep.

Never eat alphabet soup alphabetically.

I want nothing to do with natural foods. At my age I need all the preservatives I can get.

Forbidden fruit is sometimes responsible for a bad jam.

Some of today's humor is like some foods - you have to acquire a taste for it.

Most diets originate in clothing stores.

It's not the number of minutes you put in at the dining table that makes you fat; it's the seconds.

The weak will inherit the girth.

Recipe for having food taste like that which mother used to make: walk five miles before dinner.

In your work as in your food - no leftovers.

For every woman who counts her blessings, there are a hundred women who count their calories.

Movie fans who eat lots of popcorn gradually develop "bucket seats."

There is nothing wrong with my eye's. Today I killed three chocolate chips. I thought they were flies.

The trouble with people who eat like birds is that they are always chirping about it.

Here's a mystery - why is soup never spilled on a tie you don't like?

Grandma's cookies didn't need preservatives - they didn't last that long.

Beauty will not season soup.

After building a scale model, NASA scrapped its plans for installing a restaurant on the moon. They said the food turned out OK, but there just wasn't any atmosphere.

Doctors say that if you eat slowly, you will eat less. Anybody raised in a large family will tell you the same thing.

A strict diet is easy to break. As a matter of fact, it's a piece of cake.

Window sign: "We sell cake, and we sell pies, what we don't sell are thin thighs."

Good character, like good soup, is usually homemade.

Talking about your diet won't take the pounds off. You have to keep your mouth shut.

Life's little mystery - How can a two pound box of candy make you gain five pounds?

One thing is certain - more people are going on diets tomorrow than today.

I'm starting a diet tomorrow. I'm no longer going to be my blubber's keeper.

What melts in the mouth bulges in the mirror.

I'm at the age where food has taken the place of sex in my life. In fact, I've just had a mirror put over my kitchen table.

I'd give up chocolate, but I'm no quitter.

Life expectancy would grow by leaps and bounds if green vegetables smelled as good as bacon.

Wouldn't you know it, brain cells come and brain cells go, but fat cells live forever.

God provides food for every bird. He just doesn't throw it in their nests.

Now that food has replaced sex in my life, I can't even get into my own pants.

It is hard to succeed in dieting, but harder not to tell how you did it.

If you believe that you are what you eat, don't eat nuts.

Red meat is not bad for you. Now blue/green meat, that's bad for you.

If you like stirring plots, read a cookbook.

The worst kind of indigestion comes from having to eat your own words.

I only have a kitchen because it came with the house.

Warning to dieters: What's on the table soon becomes on the chair.

Forbidden fruit creates many jams.

No matter how much frosting you put on a bad cake, it is still a bad cake.

Overweight is hereditary - it shows up in your jeans.

A biscuit warms the tummy, but a smile warms the heart.

Speak sweetly; you may have to eat your words.

Eat at your own table as you would at the table of a king.

Eat slower – you will live longer.

When it's too hot in the kitchen, get out.

A good cook is one who makes meals for her family three times a day, 365 days a year, whether she cares to eat or not.

People will remember you more for the good food you serve than your 'not-so-perfect' house.

You are what you eat from your head to your feet.

Eat your bread and you'll be fed.

Lord, if you wont make me skinny, please make my friends fat.

Inquire not what boils in another's pot.

Hunger is the handmaid of Genius.

On this diet you can eat anything you want. Here's a list of the things you're allowed to want. . .

Nature apparently meant for us to sit more than walk. That's why our hips are wider than our feet

If you eat only natural organic food, you'll die healthy.

Swallowing your pride seldom leads to indigestion.

Research shows how to live longer; reduce fats and cholesterol in your diet.

Life is too short to eat brown bananas.

I have dentures, bifocals and a hearing aid, and still complain about preservatives.

If you want to know which side your bread is buttered on, just try dropping it.

Did you hear about the cookbook with a recipe for arithmetic sponge cake? You borrow all the ingredients.

Flattery is like chewing gum, enjoy it, but don't swallow it.

TEACHER: "If you had seven pieces of candy and I asked you for four of them, how many would you have left?"
LITTLE BOY: "Seven"

"My wife has tried every diet invented. Her latest is coconuts and bananas. That's all she eats."
"Is she losing weight?"
"I don't know, but she sure can climb trees."

If you want to eat less, eat alone.

Schools offer food for thought, but most students are on a diet.

Fools swallow flattery in one mouthful and drink truth drop by drop.

We get sick from what we put in our mouths, and we get hurt from what comes out of them.

Happiness

Happiness

The happiness of your life depends upon the quality of your thoughts.

Happiness is finding a $20.00 bill in your coat from last spring.

On the final analysis, all of us will be judged by the amount of happiness we have brought to others.

Those who bring happiness to the lives of others cannot keep it from themselves.

It's not your position that makes you happy—it's your disposition.

Some people cause happiness wherever they go and some people cause happiness whenever they go.

Happiness is when you drop a slice of buttered bread on the floor and it lands butter side up.

Takers eat well, givers sleep well.

Good examples have far more value than good advice.

Happiness is like a butterfly, the more you chase it, the more it will elude you. But if you turn your attention to other things, it comes softly and sits on your shoulder.

He is truly happy who has all that he wishes to have, and wishes to have nothing which he ought not to wish for.

Good words and good deeds keep life's garden free of weeds.

Happiness comes through doors you don't even know you left open.

Measure wealth not by the things you have, but by the things you have for which you would not take money.

Most folks are just about as happy as they make up their minds to be.

Happiness is when I retired and my wife burned all her credit cards.

Paths of kindness are paved with happiness.

Happiness is good at camouflage. We seek it in various places, yet it often is right at home.

Enjoyment shouldn't be postponed. There's no time like the pleasant.

Success is getting what you want. Happiness is liking what you get.

Happiness is when the baby-sitter agrees to come back a second time.

A happy person is one whose arithmetic is at its best when he's counting his blessings.

Most people ask for happiness on condition. Happiness can only be felt if you don't set any condition.

Our happiest moments are when we forget ourselves in useful effort.

Happiness is hearing that your sister-in-law, who is known as the perfect lover, just had triplets.

To me, happiness is hearing my wife speak my name in her sleep.

Happiness is a bath towel still warm from the dryer on a chilly winter morning.

Cheerfulness is one of the very best articles of dress one can wear in society.

Happiness is balancing the checkbook and finding I forgot to record a deposit.

Happiness is coming out of the mall and instantly remembering where I parked the car.

Happiness is when your neighbor takes 1600 slides of his European vacation with the lens cap on.

Try not t miss the opportunity to make others happy, even if you have to leave them alone to do it.

No matter what we are doing each day, we are all searching for happiness, even if it comes in the form of survival.

Happiness is having a loyal dog under the table when your wife cooks a new dish.

Happiness

Some people never realize what happiness is until they get married. Then it's too late.

Happiness is giving away the only thing I own – love.

Happiness, to me is seeing younger people who look older than me.

Happiness is having to prove you qualify for the 'senior' discount.

Happiness is being married to your best friend.

If you don't enjoy what you have, how could you be happier with more?

You may be able to endure sorrow alone, but happiness demands that someone share it.

Action does not always bring happiness, but there is no happiness without it.

Happiness is a quiet lover and we don't realize she has embraced us until she has gone.

Happy people are those who are too busy to notice they're happy.

Happiness is when your husband whispers in your ear, "I love you" instead of, "what's for dinner?"

Often cheerfulness is simply the capacity to ignore your unhappiness.

I don't remember ever seeing a happy man who had nothing to do.

Happiness often sneaks in through a door you didn't know you left open.

Happiness is when the car repair bill is less than the mechanic estimated.

Happiness is doing with a smile what you have to do anyway.

Most people are about as happy as they make up their minds to be.

Great Mountains of happiness grew out of little mountains of kindness.

Happiness sneaks in through a door you didn't know you left open.

Those who make others happy make themselves happy.

Happiness is like potato salad - share it with others, and it's a picnic.

The secret of happiness is not in getting more, but wanting less.

The only true happiness comes from squandering ourselves for a purpose.

Happiness is a perfume you cannot pour on others without getting a few drops on yourself.

Happy pearl divers go overboard for work.

Be thankful for what you have and be glad you didn't grow up during the Depression.

If you can't have what you want, want what you have.

If wishes were horses, we'd all take a ride.

Happiness is not a true possession until it is shared.

It's not your position in the world that will make you happy; it's your disposition.

The most important thing about the pursuit of happiness is the ability to recognize it when you catch it.

An effort made for the happiness of others lifts above ourselves.

Until one feels the spirit of Christmas, there is no Christmas.

To tidy up the house for Christmas is only a broomstick preparation. Heart preparation sweeps our lives clear. I wish we could put some of the Christmas spirit in jars and open a jar every month.

It is Christmas in the heart that puts Christmas in the air.

Christmas is not a date. It is a state of mind.

The secret of happiness is not doing what one likes, but in liking what one has to do.

Keep pretending happiness long enough and one morning you'll wake up and realize that you can hardly tell it from the real thing.

Happiness is having enough time to do something for someone else.

Some people see more in a walk around the block than others see in a trip around the world.

Happiness

Happiness is being able to fit into your old prom dress ten years later.

Happiness is hearing your husband whistle at you when you are nine months pregnant.

Happiness is the art of knowing how to do without what you can't have.

We are told that misery loves company, but happiness wants to be shared also.

The heart that is truly happy never grows old.

Anybody can be happy while busy - it's not so easy to be happy doing nothing.

Happiness is not something experienced; it's something remembered.

Happiness is the atmosphere in which all things thrive.

Health and Medicine

Health and Medicine

Good health is the thing that makes you feel that now is the best time of the year.

It is better to wear out than to rust out.

Key to longevity - Eat what you like, but less - do what you like, but more.

I went to a diet doctor and in two weeks I lost $800.

It helps our days so very much to give life's hurts the lighter touch.

Pain and suffering is inevitable but misery is optional.

Worry causes wrinkles which give you something else to worry about.

If you haven't any charity in your heart, you have the worst kind of heart trouble.

My idea of exercise is a good, brisk sit.

You never see a motorcycle parked outside a psychiatrist's office.

My doctor thinks I'm a hypochondriac. He wrote me a prescription, and when I asked the pharmacist for the generic equivalent, he handed me a bag of M&Ms.

God heals, and the doctor takes the fee.

A doctor can bury his mistakes, but an architect can only advise his clients to plant vines.

"How can I be cured?" the man asked. "Faith" said the doctor, "Hope and faith.

We now have eyeglasses for our visual problems and hearing aids for our auditory problems. If only science would come up with a thinking aid.

My doctor is one of those who puts his price list on the wall. I went in with a rare ailment, and she charged me extra for ordering off the menu.

Some people get most of their exercise running away from unpleasant tasks.

Pleasure is an unusual emotion - it seems you can get it only by giving it.

Doctor to weatherman in hospital bed, "Offhand, say you have about a 30 percent chance of recovery, increasing to 70 percent by Saturday

Your body is like a superbly tuned automobile. If you take care of it, use it wisely and maintain it properly, it will eventually break down.

When you rust when standing in the rain, you may have taken too much iron.

Doctor: I told your wife that she ought to take a holiday in Switzerland, but she seemed to think the mountain air might disagree with her."
Husband: "It wouldn't dare."

Kids give you a constant medical condition: they're either a lump in the throat, or a pain in the neck.

Some folks are not hard of hearing; they are hard of listening.

My doctor is brilliant. He told me, "With proper care, the human body will last a lifetime."

Enthusiasm is contagious. So is the lack of it.

Overheard, one patient to another in the hospital: I don't need major medical - I need a minor miracle.

In a world where death is, there is no time for hate.

An athletic person is someone who pays a teenager to mow the lawn so he can play golf or tennis to get a little exercise.

Doctors don't know everything, 50 percent of them graduated in the bottom half of their class.

Be careful about reading health books. You might die of a misprint.

Why are magazines found in the attic are so much more interesting than the same issues in the doctor's office?

Patients are not allowed to walk out of a hospital. Somebody might think they were cured.

After a hospital bill, who needs a bill?

Patience is when you listen silently to someone tell about the same operation you had.

About the only exercise some people get is running down co-workers, sidestepping responsibilities and pushing their luck.

We never know what ripples of healing we set in motion by simply smiling on one another.

Eyesight can give us vision. Insight can give us wisdom. Foresight can give us riches. Hindsight can give us ulcers.

Health insurance enables one to be ill at ease.

"My doctor said jogging could add years to my life. I think he was right. I feel ten years older already."

The difference between a rash and an allergy is about $400 worth of tests.

Today's unsung heroes are those who don't jog or work out and who don't feel guilty about it.

Nurse to obstetrician: "It's Mrs. Smith on the phone - the one you said was in false labor. She wants to know how to tie that false cord."

Three rules for healthy teeth: Brush after every meal, see your dentist often and mind your own business.

Remember when the only ones who scolded you about smoking were your parents?

It's easy to develop respiratory problems when being discharged from the hospital, that's from holding your breath while they total up your bill.

Family doctor: one who treats yours, while you support his.

Never go to a doctor whose office plants have died.

Good friends are good for your health.

Good health is the thing that makes you feel that now is the best time of the year.

A strong body makes the mind strong.

It's all right letting yourself go as long as you can let yourself back.

One of the sublime experiences we can ever have is to wake up feeling healthy after we have been sick.

Health is the first muse, and sleep is the condition to produce it.

I signed up for an exercise class and was told to wear loose-fitting clothing, if I had any loose-fitting clothing, I wouldn't have signed up in the first place!

When I was young we used to go "skinny dipping" now I just "chunky dunk."

Good health and good sense are two of life's greatest blessings.

Water is the only drink for a wise man.

After dinner sit a while, after supper walk a mile.

Gout's not just for gluttons.

Beware the young doctor and the old barber.

A man's health can be judged by which he takes two at a time - pills or stairs.

A strong positive mental attitude will create more miracles than any wonder drug.

If I'd known I was going to live this long I'd have taken better care of myself.

Health is certainly more valuable than money, because it is by health that money is procured.

My doctor gave me six months to live, but when I couldn't pay my bill he gave me six months more.

Good health is the thing that makes you feel that now is the best time of the year.

The best cure for the body is a quiet mind.

Walking is a man's best medicine.

Troubles waste the stomach like rust wastes iron.

An imaginary ailment is worse than a disease.

Many ordinary illnesses are nothing but the expression of a serious dissatisfaction with life.

It is impossible to lick your elbow, or your eyebrows.

There is no tranquilizer more effective than a few kind words.

Untold suffering seldom is.

It is better to wear out than to rust out.

I knew a man who gave up smoking, drinking, sex and food. He was healthy right up to the time he killed himself.

Doctors gave me three weeks to live. I never knew dying could be so much fun.

Hot heads and cold hearts never solved anything.

They tell you that you'll lose your mind when you grow older. What they don't tell you is that you won't miss it much.

If you feel that your doctor is unsatisfactory, remember that all medical students do not all make A's.

HEALTH TIPS:

1. Do not take things with a grain of salt, you may get high blood pressure.

2. Do not chew the fat with anyone, it may cause high cholesterol.

3. Do not hold your head up too high, it may cause cancer.

The wound of a sword will heal; the wound of a tongue will not.

Don't cut off your nose to spite your face.

A hypochondriac is someone who doesn't feel well unless he is sick.

Life is sometimes like medicine - it's good to get a second opinion.

Psychology which explains everything explains nothing, and we are still in doubt.

Do not undervalue the headache. While it is at its sharpest it seems a bad investment, but when relief begins, the unexpired remainder is worth $4.00 a minute.

When you finally get on Medicare usually your first big break will probably be a big bone.

How you lose or keep your hair depends on how wisely you choose your parents.

For fast-acting relief, try slowing down.

The only way to keep your health is to eat what you don't want, drink what you don't like and do what you'd rather not.

He who has health, has hope, has everything.

A good laugh and a long sleep are the best cures in a doctor's book.

Words are, of course, the most powerful drug used by mankind.

To get rich never risk your health. For it is the truth that health is the wealth of wealth.

A sad soul can kill you quicker than a germ.

Don't find fault, find a remedy.

Natural beauty takes at least two hours in front of the mirror.

It's considered an experimental drug because they don't know whether they'll make a bundle on it yet.

Better a lie that heals than a truth that wounds.

Never go to a surgeon who doesn't know where he lost his wedding ring.

A man went to the doctor and complained that he had trouble remembering things, so the doctor told him he would have to pay his fee in advance.

People who are always taking care of their health are like misers hording up a treasure which they never have spirit enough to enjoy.

While we are waiting for the doctor's report on our physical examination, the news of the day suddenly seems unimportant.

Health and Medicine

A woman called her doctor and said, "My son swallowed a nickel and coughed up three dimes, what should I do?"
The doctor replied, "Keep feeding him nickels."

An apple a day keeps the doctor away. So does a patient without health insurance.

Don't you just love it when the drugstore clerk traps up your aspirin, your truss, the Kaopectate, and the hemorrhoid medication, and then says, "Have a nice day!"

If it weren't for golf courses we'd never be able to find a doctor.

It's inconvenient to grow old with good health. It leaves you with so little to talk about.

Just when I can afford to lie in the sun, they decide it's hazardous to my health.

Adversity

Adversity

By its upward struggle, the fountain creates its own beauty.

In the middle of difficulty lies opportunity.

A diamond is a piece of coal that stuck to its job.

With a little, grit, the world can be your oyster.

The bubbling brook would lose its song if you removed the rocks.

A few conquer by fighting, but more battles are won by submitting.

Perseverance is what makes performers "overnight, successes" after years of trying.

We need some clouds in our life to have beautiful sunsets.

It is easier to go down a hill than up, but the best view is from the top.

A hero is one who hangs on one minute longer.

Fall seven times, stand up eight.

Preparation and enthusiasm oil the gears that help us conquer unhealthy fears.

Like a rubber band, the truth weakens the more it is stretched.

Adversity has the same effect on a man that severe training has on the pugilist - it reduces him to his fighting weight.

Even a bed of roses has thorns.

It isn't the mountains ahead that break you down, it is the grain of sand in your shoe.

Bad luck can be good luck if you learn from it.

If you don't make mistakes you might live and die without hearing your name mentioned.

Be a fault-mender rather than a fault-finder.

Never say 'Never', never say 'Always', and never give up.

If we ever got half of our wishes to come true—we'd have twice as much trouble.

Blessed are those who expect to receive nothing, for they shall never be disappointed.

No wishbone ever took the place of a backbone.

Some people, like tea, never know their real strength until they get in hot water.

One who hesitates is interrupted.

Anyone who succeeds probably has done lots of jobs the losers didn't like to do.

Perseverance is the son of patience.

God hides His blessings in adversity to surprise us with his love.

It is better to be victimized occasionally than to go through life filled with suspicion.

The best argument is that which seems merely an explanation.

You may be disappointed if you fail, but you are doomed if you don't try.

Everything has a drawback some things just draw back farther than others.

You can't escape the responsibility of tomorrow by evading it today.

We cannot direct the wind but we can adjust the sails.

If you get pushed around, you've been sending push-me-around signals.

You can break even the strongest habit by dropping it.

The trouble with being a good sport is that you have to lose to prove it.

Never deprive someone of hope; it might be all they have.

Simple solutions seldom are.

If you're sure you will never gamble again, don't bet on it.

Adversity

It's not so much the load you carry as how you carry it.

Whether you think you can or think you can't—you are right.

He whom prosperity humbles, and adversity strengthens, is the true hero.

Courage is resistance to fear, mastery of fear — not absence of fear.

To change rigor takes vigor.

To learn from our successes is wise; to learn from our failures is vital.

We are conscious of our low threshold for pain, but try to ignore our low threshold for patience.

Worry is a darkroom where fears are developed and enlarged.

One of the secrets of life is to make stepping stones out of stumbling blocks.

Abolish fear and you can accomplish whatever you wish.

You have to step backward, the better to jump forward.

Even if it burns a little bit low at times, the secret of life is to always keep the flame of hope alive.

To know the worst is peace, it is uncertainty that kills.

Very few, of us have ever drowned in our own sweat.

Courage is resistance to fear, mastery of fear — not absence of fear.

For the resolute and determined there is time and opportunity.

Peace cannot be kept by force. It can only be achieved by understanding.

It is not the going out of port, but the coming in, that determines the success of the voyage.

Keep trying. Remember the mighty oak was once little nut that stood its ground.

Man cannot discover new oceans unless he has courage to lose sight of the shore.

The best thing about trouble is its tendency to be temporary.

The difference between an error and a mistake depends on how long it takes you to correct the error.

The habit of going to the bottom of things usually lands a man on top.

People who aren't afraid to face the music may someday lead the band.

Sweat is the cologne of accomplishment.

Remember that strength is attained by meeting resistance.

By its upward struggle, the fountain creates its own beauty.

Problems can be knocked down to size depending on how you look at them.

It's not how far you fall, but how high you bounce.

Flexible people never get bent out of shape.

The bridge from challenge to reality is built with inspiration.

If you can accept losing, you can't win.

Mistakes are the portals of discovery.

Roll with the punches.

Take it with a grin, pouters never win.

If you have to swallow a toad, don't sit and look at it.

If you get burnt, just sit on the blister.

If you cannot change a thing, don't let that thing change you.

Where there's a will, there's a way.

Don't let the little worries get you down.

It never pays to worry; things have a way of working out.

Don't worry about things you can't help.

There never was a lane so long it didn't have a turn.

Adversity

Solving a problem is like a book, you have to open it before you can close it.

Don't make a mountain out of a mole hill.

He who wants a rose must respect the thorn.

Those see nothing but faults that seek for nothing else.

It is certainly wrong to despair; and if despair is wrong, hope is right.

Trust and determination will help overcome each obstacle as we meet it.

Difficulties are things that show what men are.

By trying we can easily learn to endure adversity. Another man's I mean.

There are no victories without conflict, no rainbows without storms.

He who limps is still walking.

Keep trying. You will be held up as a model to others even if you don't succeed.

If God answered everyone's prayers, the world would be filled with very old and very rich people.

We shall not see a rainbow until we put up with the rain.

The race is not always to the swift, but to those who keep running.

One thing you learn the hard way is that there is no easy way.

Accept the challenges, so that you may feel the exhilaration of victory.

If life gets a little rough around the edges, don't complain; consider that we do not reject roses because they have a few thorns.

If there were no darkness how could we appreciate the day?

Success and Failure

Success and Failure

There is only one success - to spend your life in your own way.

The two hardest things to handle in life are failure and success.

Never forget that doing what you love is the cornerstone of having success in your life.

Fear of failure becomes fear of success for those who never try anything new.

You get what you prepare for.

You can never fail in anything you try to do. You can only produce certain results.

Noah didn't wait for his ship to come in - he built one.

Some people are able to remain modest with success than others are with failure.

The road to success is always under construction.

Henry Ford once said; "Coming together is a beginning; keeping together is progress; working together is success."

Success and failure have much in common that is good. Both mean you're trying.

He who has lost confidence can lose nothing more.

Success is biting off more than you can chew, and then chewing it.

Second place just means first loser.

People who do their best today are hard people to beat tomorrow.

Great works are performed, not by strength, but perseverance. Whether you think you can or think you can't - you are right.

A pessimist is one who builds dungeons in the air.

If there's no wind, row.

Use what talents you possess; the woods would be very silent if no birds sang there except those that sang best.

If you are doing your best, you won't need any time to worry about failure.

It may be that those who do most, dream most.

Amateurs wait for inspiration, the rest of us just get up and go to work.

A goal well determined is halfway reached.

To know how to wait is the great secret of success.

The world's most destructive acid is a sour disposition.

Those who succeed in their vocations but fail as human beings can hardly be called a benefit to society.

Be sure to plan ahead—remember it wasn't raining when Noah built the ark.

Opportunity to a lazy person is like fishing—the big ones get away.

If you are going to fail, you might as well do it trying the impossible.

Success is ten per cent opportunity, and ninety percent intelligent hustle.

If you can't do great things, you can do small things in a great way.

The only people you should want to get even with are those who helped you.

Reaching high keeps people on their toes.

Make up your mind to act decidedly and take the consequences. No good is ever done in this world by hesitation.

You don't necessarily have to like your boss to work for him, you just have act like you do.

Success is a matter of staying on your toes and off other people's.

Change favors the prepared mind.

Don't be afraid to ask a dumb question—it's easier to handle than a dumb mistake.

A real failure is one that teaches us nothing.

The only way to avoid making a mistake is to do nothing.

Only the electric company has the power to make everyone see the light.

Always beat the wall louder than the drummer in the next apartment.

A good reason is a good excuse, but an excuse is not always a good reason.

The reward of a thing well done is often to have it done.

The big winners are invariably men who have snatched success from the jaws of failure.

The person who makes a success of living is the one who sees his goal steadily and aims for it unswervingly.

You can never get to second base if you keep your foot on first.

Today's opportunity: To care enough to dry a tear, to dare enough to volunteer, to live that others may he blessed, to give our talents and our best.

A runner without a leg to stand on will find another way to get around.

Why should anyone criticize a committee if he or she hasn't done a thing.

Difficulties are not difficult to bear if they make you better, not bitter.

Rainmaking isn't all that difficult, just plan a picnic or wash your car.

The art of winning in business lies in working hard, and not taking the game to seriously.

The haves and haves nots can often be traced to the dids and did nots.

The person who makes no mistakes does not usually make anything.

Those who say "Work well done never, never needs redoing" never weeded a garden.

If you don't have time to do it right, when will you have time to do over?

At first you might believe you could, then you might believe you couldn't—you'd be right both times.

A genius is a person who aims at something no one else can see and hits it.

Opportunity is a mischievous old dame. She gives us a few invitations but often camouflages them.

Ants can carry 20 times their own weight, which is useful information if you need help moving a potato chip cross town.

You either make dust or eat dust.

Talent wins games, but teamwork and intelligence wins championships.

We need to learn to set our course by the stars, not by the lights of every passing ship.

You can't base your life on other people's expectations.

Only those who risk going too far will ever know how far they can go.

A goal is a dream with a deadline.

How to tell a winner from a loser-- a winner credits his winning to "good luck", even though it wasn't. A loser blames his "bad luck" even though it wasn't.

It doesn't do any good to sit up and take notice if you keep on sitting.

People forget how fast you did a job, but they remember how well you did it.

The successful man will profit from his mistakes and try again in a different way.

Opportunity dances with those already on the dance floor.

Hard work spotlights the character of people: Some turn up their sleeves, some turn up their noses, and many don't turn up at all.

Success is never final, and failure is never fatal; it's courage that counts.

Every great accomplishment starts with the decision to try.

Success is the maximum utilization of the ability that you have.

Rather fail with honor than succeed by fraud.

It is better to deserve honors and not have them than to have them and not deserve them.

The chief factor in any man's success or failure must be his own character.

Most people would succeed in small things if they were hot troubled by great ambitions.

Even the woodpecker owes his success to the fact that he uses is head and keeps pecking away until he finishes the job he starts.

The difference between hard work end luck is that hard work doesn't run out.

Success seems to be largely a matter of hanging on after others have let go.

Great opportunities are the ordinary ones you work on.

Those who apply themselves too closely to little things often become incapable of great things.

Opportunity is a mischievous old dame. She gives us a few invitations but often camouflages them.

The secret of joy in work is contained in one word - excellence.

To know how to do something well is to enjoy it.

Complete success alienates a man from his fellows, but suffering makes kinsmen of us all.

Hot is hot only when you have cold to compare it with.

Usually a workaholic never slows down long enough to let opportunity catch up with him.

People who believe in success at any cost usually end up paying a very high price.

The man who removes a mountain begins by carrying away small stones.

The harder you work the harder it is to surrender.

Choose a job you love, and you will never have to work a day in your life.

Often the difference between a successful person and a failure is which one got tired first.

Ambition never gets anywhere until it forms a partnership with work.

If you make a mistake, don't make another one by making excuses for it.

It's easier to make up your mind when you learn what the boss thinks.

Success doesn't spoil anybody who wasn't a little rotten to begin with.

Winners watch for opportunities; losers wait for lucky breaks.

Success in almost any field depends more on energy and drive than it does on intelligence.

In order to succeed, we must first believe that we can.

There is no elevator to success; you have to take the stairs.

The key to failure is trying to please everybody.

A man can succeed at almost anything for which he has unlimited enthusiasm.

All serious daring starts from within.

Once you have missed the first buttonhole, you'll never manage to button up.

We could take a lesson from the weather; it pays no attention to criticism.

You haven't failed until you give up.

If you think something is impossible don't interrupt those who are getting it done.

The secret of business success is to keep your head up and your overhead down.

The rules of success won't work unless you do.

Success is built on the ability to do better than good enough.

True success is overcoming they fear of being unsuccessful.

There is no failure except in no longer trying.

The greatest artist was once a beginner.

The doors of opportunity are marked 'push' and 'pull'.

Success breeds confidence, but confidence also breeds success.

Those who never accept fault can never improve.

Failure isn't falling down, it's staying there after you've hit the bottom.

It takes as much courage to have tried and failed as it does to have tried and succeeded.

The individual activity of one person with backbone will do more than a thousand with mere wishbone.

People with goals succeed because they know where they are going.

If you want some good thing, picture it, believe it, until it becomes your real desire.

It doesn't do any good to sit up and take notice if you just keep on sitting.

If you get to thirty-five and your job still involves wearing a name tag, you've probably made a serious vocational error.

All that you do, do with your might.

Success is when your name is in everything but the phone book.

I am a great believer in luck, and the harder I work the more I have of it.

When you come to the end of your rope, tie a knot and hang on.

Many of life's failures are people who did not realize how close they were to success when they gave up.

It is easier to climb the ladder of success if dad owns the ladder factory.

For people who want to succeed in life, some four letter words you may use successfully are - work, risk, guts and zest.

When a job is once begun - never leave it - 'til it's done

Be the labor great or small - do it well or not at all.

If the job's worth doing, it's worth doing right.

If it's your best, it is the BEST.

Never start anything you don't expect to finish.

Don't do the dreaded job last, but first, so you can have the rest of the day to look forward to.

Make fun out of work, it goes a lot better and faster.

The beginning is the most important part of the work.

Who will pull the wagon if we all get in to ride?

Put away your "can't" and use your hands.

Many hands make light work.

The road to success is always under construction.

Greatness grows from a pile of small accomplishments.

It's the steps forward that get you to your destination.

Sometimes we get farther, standing still.

If you are lost you need to change directions.

The progress of rivers to the ocean is not so rapid as that of man to error.

Failure is not our only punishment for laziness; There is also the success of others.

If all the good people were clever, and all the clever people were good, the world would be nicer than ever we thought it possibly could.

Wrong must not win by technicalities.

If I were to begin life again, I should want it as it was. I would only open my eyes a little more.

Be not simply good; be good for something.

If you have one thing that you can do well, you're doing well.

Ideas are funny little things - they won't work unless you do.

Six essential qualities that are the key to success: Sincerity, personal integrity, humility, courtesy, wisdom, charity.

Success and Failure

Success is relative - whenever you have it, you'll have relatives.

The world pays a salary for what you know wages for what you do.

The best solution to a problem is always prevention.

You snooze. You lose.

Remember that winners do what losers don't want to do.

The difference between a job and a career is often one's attitude.

Did you ever notice that people who fail seem to believe in luck a whole lot more than people who succeed?

Some people go through piling one success on top of another without taking time out to enjoy any of them.

Enthusiasm keeps you going, but it is competence that keeps you winning.

Talent is knowing how to do something; Judgment is knowing whether to do it.

It doesn't matter who pays your salary; you are always working for yourself.

Failure comes from following the line of least persistence.

An idea is a curious thing - it won't work unless you do.

All great accomplishments have a simple beginning.

Inspiration comes from working every day.

Enthusiasm is the element of success in everything. It robs endurance of difficulty and makes pleasure of duty.

Opportunity is like a dial tone. It's there. All it requires is a little push.

Great things have been accomplished by folks who didn't try a bit harder - just longer.

Failures are more commonly caused by having no choice than wrong decisions.

The loser often is someone who tried almost as hard as the winner.

An opportunist is somebody who does what you were going to do, one of these days.

That you'll never reach perfection is no excuse for aiming at less.

If you always predict you'll do less well than you're capable of doing, you're not being modest, you're just protecting yourself from failure. And you're guaranteeing that you'll never really succeed.

To love what you do and feel it matters - how could anything be more fun?

All change is not growth, as all movement is not forward.

Destiny is not a matter of chance, it is a matter of choice.

The reward of a thing well done is to have done it.

The world is always ready to receive talent with open arms.

If faith can move mountains, imagine what hard work can do.

There is no compensation for work that can equal the love of doing it.

Never go up a ladder with just one nail.

Confidence comes from experience - experience comes from know-how.

The greatest power that a person possesses is the power to choose.

All dreams come true if we have the courage to pursue them.

No matter what you undertake, you will never do it until you think you can.

Don't judge those who try and fail. Judge only those who fail to try.

Opportunity and temptation are different. The first one knocks, and the second one invites itself in.

Action is the difference between why and why not.

It's wise to remember that success is not a permanent condition.

A successful person is one who looks to the future with one eye on the past, and the other eye on the present.

All progress is due to the fact that somebody had a vision of something better.

Success is the ability to get along with some people and ahead of others.

Victories often occur after you see no way to succeed, but refuse to give up anyway.

Perhaps the best way to lend some people a hand is to give them a well-placed foot.

It's the job that's never started that takes longest to finish.

The problem with doing nothing is not knowing when you're finished.

The greatest danger for most of us is that our aim is too high and we miss, but that our aim is too low and we reach it.

I always say, "don't make plans, make options."

Always bear in mind that your own resolution to succeed is more important than any one thing.

Success is never final, but failure can be.

Life

Life

Enjoy life - This is not a rehearsal.

Life is like a bath---the longer you stay in it, the more wrinkled you get

There are three stages of life - youth, middle age, and "You're looking well."

Life is like a bicycle, you don't fall off unless you stop pedaling.

Make the most of all that comes and the least of all that goes.

To stay youthful, stay useful.

Nothing is half as tiring as the eternal shadow of unfinished work.

Life is what you make of it—kind of like Play-Doh.

It takes two to lie - one to lie and one to listen.

What a world - everybody asks how you're feeling and then acts bored when you begin to tell them.

If God hadn't intended us to be happy, he wouldn't have made it so easy for us to smile.

You can live here in this world only once, but if you live right, once is enough.

Character is not what you are thought to be, but are.

Those who convert dreams into reality have done the most to advance civilization.

If the facts don't fit the theory, change the facts.

Life doesn't require that we be the best, only that we try our best.

Let us be of good cheer, remembering that the misfortunes hardest to bear are those which never come.

A pessimist takes life with a grain of sulk.

People are not masters of the planet, only guests.

Count your life by smiles not tears, count you age by friends, not years.

There are two kinds of people who don't say much—those who are quiet and those who talk a lot.

The trouble with being punctual is that nobody is there to appreciate it.

In life most of the mountains we climb we built ourselves.

The smallest good deed is better than the greatest good intention.

Every person cannot be the best, but every person can be his or her best.

I believe that the first test of a truly great man is his humility.

Only you can be yourself, on one else is qualified for the job.

Those persons who are always dog-tired like to growl about it.

When you get up and go has gotten up and gone, you've reached old age.

The naked truth is more appealing when it's pressed in a smile.

Looking at the bright side of things will improve, not damage, your insight.

All our dreams can come true, if we have the courage to pursue them.

The easiest thing to keep in your head is a cold.

Life is 10 percent what to me and 90 percent how I react to it.

The state of your life is nothing more than a reflection of your state of mind.

The truth is if one of us succeeds, we all do.

Keep a solid picture of the task you want to accomplish in your mind, and refuse to let that intention disappear.

I can keep a secret—but those I tell it to never can.

Nothing great in the world has been accomplished without passion.

Life

Age and treachery will always overcome youth and skill. Conniving and brilliance only come with age and experience,

Aging seems to be the only available way to live a long life.

It is better to look ahead and prepare than to look back and regret.

The smallest light is seen in the darkest night.

One of the heaviest pieces of baggage to carry through life is a chip on the shoulder.

The nice thing about being imperfect is the joy it brings to others.

Nature creates ability; luck provides it with opportunities.

We must always have old memories and young hopes.

Life is not a problem to be solved, but a gift to be enjoyed.

Tough times never last, tough people do.

People get most tired when they are standing still.

The only people who find what they are looking for in life are the fault finders.

When a man is wrapped up in himself, he makes a pretty small package.

Life is what we make it—always has been always will be.

They say such nice things about people at their funerals that it makes me sad to realize I'm going to miss mine by just a few days.

Those who know how to enjoy life are not poor.

Life's greatest challenge is keeping your weight down and your spirits up.

Old age is like a rocket launching - at a certain stage, you count down.

What is a computer's first sign of old age? Loss of memory.

The memories we collect and give brighten our lives as long as we live.

Remember the years, but forget the tears.

A moment's insight is sometimes worth a life's experience.

It is difficult to have rosy thoughts of the future when your mind is full of the blues of the past.

Good, better, best—never let rest until good is better and better is best.

Life is a continuous process of getting used to the things we hadn't expected.

Success in life comes not from holding a good hand, but in playing a poor hand well.

People who sing their own praises are apt to be soloists.

Courage is very important. Like a muscle, it's strengthened by use.

In youth we learn, in old age we understand.

The best way to lighten life's load is by lifting a weight off somebody else's back.

One cannot say he has lived unless he has helped another to do so.

No man is a failure who is enjoying life.

Life may be like a game of cards; we cannot help the hand that is dealt us, but we can help the way we play it.

In the game of life, it's easier to see the goalposts if you keep your chin up.

Life is tough after the kids leave home and you have no one to blame for things but each other.

Life is like riding a bicycle, you don't fall off unless you stop pedaling.

Vitality! That's the pursuit of life, isn't it?

Life is not a problem to be solved, but a gift to be enjoyed.

Hope sees the invisible, feels the intangible, and achieves the impossible.

Life is a great big canvas and you should throw all the paint on it you can.

Life is a choice of values.

Shoot for the moon even if you miss it, you will land among the stars.

Life

To overlook the little things in life is to miss the biggest part of life itself.

Life can be understood by looking backward, but it must be lived by looking forward.

Life is like a roll of toilet paper. The closer it gets to the end, the faster it goes.

The less of routine, the more of life.

Don't just live and let live, but live and help live.

What counts in life is what we do for others.

The hardest thing to learn in life is which bridge to cross and which to burn.

Life is not a problem to be solved, but a gift to be enjoyed.

It's choice, not chance, that determines your destiny.

If you want the rainbow, you have to put up with the rain.

Just as important as WHAT happens to you in this life is HOW you take it.

Courage and faith, modesty and humor are the keys to life's doors.

Don't leave God out of your life.

Make yourself useful as well as ornamental.

Life is what happens to you when you're making other plans.

Need, by nature, is the same - no matter how or to whom it came.

Fit yourself into accord with the things into which it has been your lot to have been cast.

People who cut themselves off from God are left with only frail human resources to live by.

Life is a picture - paint it well.

Many talented persons drift aimlessly through life; a purpose will give true meaning for living.

Tame the savageness of man and make gentle the life of the world.

No one can hinder you from saying or doing what is in accordance to Nature.

Life is short, art long, opportunity fleeting, experience treacherous, judgment difficult.

Life is too important to be taken seriously.

Playing golf is different from life - in golf you try to get into a hole, and in life you don't have to try.

Giving up on yourself is a crime--and it carries a life sentence.

Fill your life with experiences not excuses.

Every good thought you think is contributing its share to the ultimate result of your life.

Those whom we support hold us up in life.

If I end up disappointed with my life, it'll be because of what I've done, not failed to do.

One of the problems with living on the edge is that there is so very little room for error.

Anyone who keeps the ability to see beauty never grows old.

There's only one thing more painful than learning from experience, and that is learning from experience.

Do you ever feel like life is a car wash and you're going through it on a bicycle?

Things in life even out pretty well. Others people's troubles are not as bad as ours, but their children are a lot worse.

To know that even one life has breathed easier because you have lived. This is to have succeeded.

It seems to me that the only hell a man needs is to have his eyes opened to the man he might have been.

Remember that life is not measured in hours, but in accomplishments.

Life

One of life's greatest pleasures is coming up to your illegally parked car and not finding a ticket on it.

There are lights and shadows that make your life deep and strong.

It's a funny thing about life: If you refuse to accept anything but the best, you very often get it.

An acre of performance is worth a whole world of promises.

Have faith in what you believe and don't give up on the future. Today's dream is the threshold of tomorrow's discovery.

More things grow in the garden than the gardener sows.

Self-esteem is feeling good about yourself, regardless of the facts.

The meaning of life is to make your own life meaningful.

The pleasure you get from life is equal to the attitude you put into it.

I look back on my life like a good day's work.

Bert's Observations

Observations

Sometimes the heart sees what is invisible to the eye.

You are the only person on this earth who can use your ability.

Anger is never without a reason, but seldom with a good one.

He that won't be counseled, can't he helped.

Be civil to all; sociable to many; familiar with few; friend to one; enemy to none.

Necessity never made a good bargain.

To be humble to superiors is duty, to equals courtesy, to inferiors nobleness

I make mistakes, of course, but I do not respond to encores.

Self-control means staying cool while others are trying to make it hot for you.

Hold faithfulness and sincerity as first principles.

It is a pleasure to give advice, humiliating to need it, and perfectly normal to ignore it.

The shallowest stream usually makes the loudest noise.

Prejudice is a matter of being down on something you're not up on.

Overheard - My wife is so ugly I take her everywhere I go because I can't stand to kiss her goodbye.

One woman to another: "Why don't you go to him in a perfectly straight forward way and lie about the whole thing?"

I found something that does the job of five men - one woman.

Fashion is a strange thing - designers make a mistake, and millions of women pay for it.

Confucius say: Lovers in triangle not on square.

Have you ever wondered how real men knew they were real men before they invented pickup trucks, beer, and baseball?

A consultant is a caboose with delusions of being a locomotive.

Ever notice that some people are very sensitive, but only to their own needs?

Perhaps the secret of modern life is to try and make a little gain on the good days and hope to break even on the bad days.

Get-up-and-go is a quality lacked by most bores.

Q,: What is a buccaneer?
A: Too much to pay for corn.

When you're young, you want to be the master of your fate and the captain of your soul. When you're old, you'll settle for being master of your weight and captain of your bowling team.

Trust everybody, but cut the cards.

Each of us decides to be an optimist or a pessimist, a builder or a belittler, a giver or a grasper.

Some schools enforce a strict rule on sports; No athlete is awarded a letter unless he can tell which letter it is.

To know what is right and not to do it is the worst cowardice.

Those who got what they want too easily end up crying out for the impossible.

Forgiveness is the sweetest revenge.

I never have any pity for conceited people, because I think they carry comfort about with them.

The electric chair was invented by a dentist.

Whoever coined the phrase "it's only a game" probably just lost one.

A bore is a person who talks when you want him to listen.

NEWSPAPER AD: "For sale: Six dresses, size 10, never worn. So much for positive thinking.

Watching some TV shows makes a person wonder what the networks rejected.

There's one thing in favor of real life - it takes your mind off all that suffering on TV.

No word in the English language rhymes with month.

To understand what little chance you have of changing others, just think of changing yourself.

It's physically impossibly for you to lick your elbow.

"Go" is the shortest complete sentence in the English language.

Cross-country skiing is great if you live in a small country.

A man who lives by himself and for himself is apt to be corrupted by the company he keeps.

Those who don't have the right spirit don't have a ghost of a chance of succeeding.

There's nothing duller than an old blade trying to be sharp.

Conceit is equivalent to all other sins.

Golf is the game that turned the cows out of the pasture and let the bull in.

The only thing different between a rut and a groove is often your frame of mind.

It is a great pleasure to do a good deed in secret and have it found out by accident.

The Menendez brothers, after shooting both their parents are asking for mercy on the grounds that they are orphans.

The best kind of workmen's compensation is recognition on the job.

What we call results are beginnings.

Malicious gossip can be as dangerous as lightning and as destructive as tornadoes.

Why did the moron take a ladder to the bar?
A: Because he heard the drinks wore on the house.

Did you hear about the street cleaner who was fired for dreaming? He couldn't keep his mind in the gutter.

Self-praise usually is a solo.

What do you get if you cross poison ivy with a four leaf clover?
A rash of good luck.

I ran across Ivana Trump's new novel at the bookstore. I couldn't miss it. It was the only one with a mink jacket.

I love Thanksgiving. Almost everyone seems to be in the spirit. Just today another driver called me a "turkey" and I told him to "stuff it."

Judge, "Young man, this is the fifth time this month you've appeared before me."
Defendant, "Your Honor, when I find someone I admire, I like to give him all my business."

Middle age makes its appearance when a man who was a human dynamo starts showing signs of ignition trouble.

Affections cannot keep their youth any more than men.

If your conscience never bothers you, you're either doing every thing right or something very wrong.

I smile because I have no idea what's going on!

Sign in Beauty Shop: You can't keep from aging, but you can dye in the attempt.

Fashion is something that goes in one year and out the other.

The trouble with many people who object to doing a full day's work is they're such conscientious objectors.

Nobody cares if you can't dance well. Just get up and dance,

The nice thing about being a celebrity is that when you bore people they think it's their fault.

Don't sweat the pretty things and don't pet the sweaty things.

One tequila, two tequila, three tequila, floor.

If someone with multiple personalities threatens to kill himself, is it considered a hostage situation?

Someone broke a hole the nudist colony fence. Cops looking into it.

A perfectionist takes pains to do everything just right and in taking pains, he gives them to everyone in sight.

The best answer to anger is silence.

No one has a better command of language than the person who knows just when to talk and when to keep quiet.

Sometimes "common sense" doesn't seem to be too common.

The words, "it's none of my business" should be a complete sentence.

Some football players stay in college for five years or more. They can run and kick, but they can't pass.

An optimistic point of view will always look much better on you.

Hate the sin but love the sinner.

Strong coffee doesn't pour - it seems to slide out of the pot.

Weep not peeling other people's onions.

Do not go out of your way to do good, but do good whenever it comes in your way.

Good habits are the mentors that regulate our lives.

Beautiful young people are accidents of nature's heart; but beautiful old people are really works of art.

Honesty doesn't need fine print.

It is better to forget and smile than to remember and be sad.

If you have a job without aggravations, you don't have a job.

People who quote scripture usually quote the parts they like.

Customer to snippy waitress: "What's a girl like you doing in a nice place like this?

A pessimist is a man who has been compelled to live with an optimist.

Old boys have their playthings as well as young ones; the difference is only the price.

To serve the public faithfully, and at the same time to please it entirely, is impracticable.

It is better to be only sometimes right than to be at all times wrong.

You can not reform a man who has a great many little faults, but no big ones.

Think less about your rights, more about your duties.

Parties who fuss about saving their souls, probably have no souls worth saving.

When a church becomes fashionable it ceases to be the house of God.

It is better to be stupid like everyone than to be clever like no one.

Nightly outing - Her teeth are like stars, so shining and bright.
Like those up above, they're out every night.

Words cannot change the truth. Being in the right does not depend on having a loud voice.

We judge ourselves by what we feel capable of doing, while others judge us by what we have already done.

Humility is a strange thing - The minute you think you've got it, you've lost it.

Worry is an old man with bended head, carrying a load of feathers which he thinks is lead.

"Security, comfort" - How often we hear these words today? What about obligation, responsibility?

There is usually more ego than desire to help in criticism.

It takes you to make an argument.

The most impractical gift you can give anyone is a piece of your mind.

A person may be very secretive and yet have no secrets.

The ideas that benefit a man are seldom welcomed by him on first presentation.

A gentleman is one whose virtues are not founded on self-interest.

No person utterly miserable ever did a great work.

An ounce of performance is worth a pound of preachment.

Courage comes only to those who have done the thing before.

No choice is also a choice.

The sad part about people who try to lead a model life is that you can tell they're only posing.

When a man won't listen to his conscience, it's usually because he doesn't want advice from a total stranger.

Experience is not what happens to a man; it is what a man does with what happens to him.

Many people look more intelligent wearing eyeglasses, but that can he merely an optical illusion.

There are no degrees of honesty.

A compliment without enthusiasm is like champagne that has gone flat.

Did you hear about the ex-miss America who opened up a housecleaning service? She called it "Sweeping Beauty."

A smart girl is one who knows how to play tennis, piano, and dumb.

If you were to list the nicest half dozen people you know, who would the other five be?

The secret of contentment is knowing how to enjoy what you have, and to be able to lose all desire for things beyond your reach.

Change is a challenge to adventurous, and opportunity to the alert, and a threat to the insecure.

The best way to get even is to forget.

Impossible things are simply those which so far have never been done.

The reward of a good deed is to have done it,

The best remedy for decay is an active interest in human affairs.

Some people will hold anything except their tongues, keep anything except their word, and lose nothing except their patience.

The worst thing in life is not getting your heart's desire; the second worst thing is getting it.

If you can remain calm, you don't have all the facts.

That's like asking Mrs. Abe Lincoln—"Aside from that", how was the play?

I am an equal opportunity hugger!

Sometimes the most imaginative thing at the local movie theater is the refreshment display in the lobby.

I may have my faults, but being wrong isn't one of them.

Why is it called Alcoholics Anonymous when the first thing you do is stand up and say, "My name is Clyde, and I am an alcoholic?"

You know you are a member of the jet set when your second car is a yacht.

A gossip is someone who peddles a juicy tidbit, a non-gossip is someone who hasn't heard it yet.

You get a hint of the country's junk mail problem when even postmen refer to themselves as litter carriers.

To err is human - but it feels divine.

A compliment is something like a kiss through a veil.

The difference between a cat and a comma is that a cat has claws at the end of paws, and a comma has a pause at the end of a clause.

Many overcomers have earned the degree, "Doctor or Difficulties" at the university of Hard Knocks.

Just because someone has fancy sneakers doesn't mean they can run faster.

The reason that some people judge a book by its cover is that they don't want to take the time to read it.

Bert's Observations

Life isn't always fair; fortunately, however, neither is the weather.

Invitation to a teacher's retirement party: "You are cordially invited to attend a party for a woman who no longer has any class or principals.

Many of the people who go on ego trips don't carry too much luggage.

I have an impersonal trainer. We meet at the gym, we don't talk, he works out alone and I go home.

There's no pillow as soft as a clear conscience.

I often marvel how it is that though each man loves himself beyond all else, he should yet value his own opinion of himself less than that of others.

In matters of principle, stand like a rock; in matters of taste, swim with the current.

Patience is the ability to idle your motor when you feel like stripping your gears.

It was a face that had nothing to fear. Everything had been done to it that anybody could think of.

You should always turn a frown into a smile, even if you have to stand on your head to do it.

One nice thing about egotists; they don't talk about other people.

The best liar is he who makes the smallest amount of lying go the longest way.

Always remember that you get the angriest at the people you care the most about.

Never take a knife to a gun fight.

A bore is someone who talks when you want to talk.

When you're all out of brilliance, dazzle them with enthusiasm.

Anger is never without a reason, but seldom with a good one.

In an ideal world, all machines would function perfectly except the bathroom scales.

When it comes to giving, some people will stop at nothing.

It is a great mistake for men to give up saying what is charming, they give up thinking what is charming.

Sanity lies in your ability to think individually and act collectively.

Cease being a creature, and become a creator.

Logic is one thing, and commonsense another.

Morality is simply the attitude we adopt towards people we personally dislike.

No idea is ever dead until those who believe in it say it's dead.

Anger is never without a reason, but seldom with a good one.

A man's life is dyed the color of his imagination.

The biggest crooks in the world are the guys who start a conversation. "To be perfectly honest" or "to be absolutely Frank".

It's interesting how the things that other people do seem so horrible, and yet when you're doing them they seem so right.

No matter what happens, there is always someone who knew it would.

Some winter mornings are so cold, cars won't start running and noses won't stop.

Whoever said oil and water don't mix never went to the beach on a hot day.

Once uttered, words run faster than horses.

Gossip is that which goes in both ears and, comes out of the mouth greatly enlarged.

Praise the soil in which joy thrives.

The important thing about your lot in life is whether you use it for parking or building.

Don't discourage another person's plan unless you have a better one.

Even back in Grandpa's time there was something to make you sleep. They called it work.

Bert's Observations

We work so hard to keep our outside presentable when the inside is what matters.

An apology is the super glue of life, it can repair just about anything.

Society talks about the need for exercise while it invents the touch telephone and the remote control for television.

Lady to saleswoman: Can I try on that dress in the window? No, you have to try it on in the dressing room.

He that rises late must trot all day.

Every man has three characters: That which he exhibits, that which he has, and that which he thinks he has.

Always listen with deft ears.

Q: Why do basketball players have bad table manners?
A: Because they are always dribbling.

Man is the only creature on earth who can reason and be unreasonable.

Common sense is the most widely shared commodity in the world, for every man is convinced that he is well-supplied with it.

We're likely to think of folks as having different abilities when what they have is different amounts of determination.

The world only exists in your eyes - your conception of it. You can make it as big or as small as you want to,

Flattery is all right - if you don't inhale;

If you're going to get caught in the act, make sure it's an act of kindness.

He who gets too big for his britches will he exposed in the end.

When you are angry or frustrated, what comes out? Whatever it is, it's a good indication of what you're made of.

Anger is hurt turned inside out.

If you'd like company to drop in, just leave the house messy.

Things are not always better because of change, but they never get better without change.

A lady is a woman who makes a man behave like a gentleman.

Things could he worse. Suppose daytime soap operas ran Saturdays and Sundays, too.

One of life's greatest temptations is the urge to leave the price tag on an expensive gift you are giving.

It's always easier to find a silver lining in someone else's cloud.

When we clean out the useless things from our attic, maybe we should do the same thing to our minds.

What's so unbelievable about communicating with the dead? Schoolteachers have been doing it for years.

It takes a lot of perseverance on your part to try to be a perfectionist, and even more tolerance on the part of others.

You can always tell when a man is well informed; his views are pretty much like your own.

Hate is like acid, it can damage the vessel in which it is stored as well as destroy the object on which it is poured.

Advice is like medicine - you have to take it to see if it does any good.

Never drive faster than your angel can fly.

A positive attitude may just annoy enough people to make it worth your while.

Give your troubles to God; He will be up all night anyway.

The ideal guest is one who gets homesick before your bedtime.

Patience is the power to idle your engines when you feel more like stripping your gears.

You should never take the attitude of 'let someone else do it' unless you're getting a haircut.

Have you heard about the workaholic? He was charged with resisting a rest.

Envy is the sorrow of fools.

People who are busybodies usually don't have much to do.

It is the good girls who keeps the diaries: the bad girls never have time.

An honest man's word is as good as his bond.

The superior man is dignified, but not proud, the inferior man is proud, but not dignified.

I don't need snubs to keep me modest, one glance at my license photo is enough to keep me humble.

You'll learn the art of conversation isn't dead the next time you stand waiting for a public telephone.

It is often better not to see an insult than to avenge it.

To be good is noble, but to teach others how to he good is nobler - and less trouble.

Deal with honor and sleep at night.

On his tombstone: "Here lies *Harry* Houdini - we think."

Every afternoon, a young boy named Giovanni rushed to Michelangelo's studio to watch the famous sculptor chip away at a 14 foot high block of marble. Week after week the boy sat by and silently watched in wonder as the magnificent form of David began to take shape. When the statue was finally done, the boy asked in amazement, "How did you know he was in there?"

Any one who drives like the devil may soon meet him.

Mean what you say or you demean what you say.

To go beyond is as wrong as to fall short.

Dear Ted: I now realize that you are the only one I ever really loved. I'm sorry. Can you ever forgive me for leaving you? I didn't mean to avoid you: I just needed some time and space to get my life in order. Please call me soon. We had so much going for us, and I want to try again. Until then, know that I'll always love you. Lovingly, Linda
PS Congratulations on winning the lottery.

On the fourth day of Christmas my true love gave to me: four calling birds, three French hens, two turtledoves, and a lawsuit from the ASPCA.

OVERHEARD: "The elderly couple next door are going to sell their home and buy one of those pandemonium's."

Good judgment is what you think a person has if he trusts yours.

Good manners never hurt anyone, but some folks apparently think they do by the way they avoid using them.

It's a strange world, we've got mobile homes that don't move, sports clothes to work in, junk food that costs more than the real thing, and sweatshirts to loaf in.

For prying into any human affairs, none are equal to those whom it does not concern.

Tolerance is an agreement to tolerate intolerance.

Any system can be defeated by one single man who places himself out of harmony with it.

A man's measure is his ability to select men and materials and organize them.

People who are wrong seem to talk louder than anyone else.

Don't bemoan the incompetence of others; their possession of it is what makes you look good.

A church may be just what's required, if a "faith lift" is what is desired.

There is no point is speaking unless you can improve on silence.

I don't like these new hotels. Their towels are so big. It makes it hard to close my suitcase.

Rain won't do any good unless the sun comes out - nor will criticism if there is no praise.

Memory is a marvelous thing; it enables you to remember a mistake each time you repeat it.

When Samuel Goldwyn learned that a friend's newborn son would he named Bill, be said. "Bill? Every Tom, Dick and Harry is named Bill."

My aunt is an incredible pack rat. She never throws anything away. She's so had about it that I've been afraid to visit her since Uncle Harry died.

These are funny times. The other day I bought a wastebasket and carried it borne in a plastic bag. As soon as I got home, I put the plastic bag in the wastebasket.

The test is this: Which do you love most, Victory or Truth?

A man possessing initiative is a creator.

A wise man does not need advice, and a fool will not take it.

To repeat an unkind truth is just as bad as to invent a lie.

Character is fine tuned by the amount of criticism you can take and the amount you can forgive.

How do you get a man to do sit-ups?
Put the remote control between his toes

If something goes without saying, it's best to let it.

During the Renaissance, they believed one man could possess the sum total of human knowledge. Today, it takes two teenagers and a cab driver.

We're looking for someone who is responsible, explained the personnel manager. "Perfect!" responded the job applicant. "Everywhere I've worked, whenever something went wrong, they always said I was responsible."

Nobody in the history of the United States ever bought a fruitcake for himself.

Scientist have just determined that the rings around Saturn are made up entirely of lost luggage.

The airlines have been extremely careful lately to make sure t he person sitting next to each emergency exit is strong enough to open it. I just hope the person I'm sitting next to is strong enough to open my bag of peanuts.

How do you know those are my leaves that blew into your yard?

Christmas candy and toy frontiers
now ride in the sleds of our financiers.

Cars today are still built for speed. They go through 3-minute car washes, 10 minute oil changes, and 60-minute parking meters.

It is difficult not to believe in a Supreme Being when we hear a baby laugh or see the tree leaves turn color in the autumn.

Wouldn't it be a better world if everybody was as pleasant as the person who's trying to borrow something from you?

I'm at my sexual peak, and let me tell you it's lonely at the top.

About the time we catch up with our neighbors, they refinance.

You never realize how speed-conscious Americans are until you see a crowd of then trying to go through a revolving door.

I asked my waiter, "What is the soup dujour? He said he'd have to check. Finally be came back and said, "It's the soup of the day."

My brother is little too devoted t his car. After he washes it, he dabs a little perfume behind each tire.

Schools out and there they are, screeching and giggling and tearing up homework. Wouldn't you think teachers would act more dignified?
The quickest way to lose your shirt is to put too much on the cuff.

Nowadays people speak their minds on T-shirts.

Why do people who want to drown their sorrows always look for someone to go swimming with them?

Early to bed and early to rise may make a man healthy, wealthy and wise, but it also makes him a lousy house guest.

Sex is a misdemeanor. The more I miss, de meaner I get.

If push comes to shove, have a citizen's arrest, not a cardiac arrest.

The trouble with a skeleton in the closet is, it will not stay there.

I don't care what color my hair turns as long as it doesn't turn loose.

A TV weatherman received the following call from an irate viewer: "You may be interested in knowing that I have just shoveled through six feet of fair and warmer from my driveway.

Honey will you come change the channel on the TV? There's a physical fitness program I want to see.

Many of the people who claim they want to get back to nature would probably change their minds once they really got there.

And to my wife, who hated my guts, I leave my large intestine.

A woman is never more cunning than when she is deliberately playing dumb.

Technology has made the world a neighborhood. Now we have to make it a brotherhood.

If Rip Van Winkle were alive today and slept for 20 years, think of the thousands of messages he'd have on his answering machine.

The bathtub was invented in 1850 and the telephone in 1875. If you had been living in 1850, you could have sat in the tub for 25 years without the phone ringing once.

If you really want the world to beat a path to your door, try taking a nap.

Swimming is good exercise and it reminds people of the importance of keeping their mouths shut.

Sometimes when you're trying to get both ends to meet, somebody moves the ends.

Everyone hears strange noises. A small child hears scary sounds coming from under the bed. An adult hears them coming from under the hood of the car.

Lots of things that people won't be able to do without haven't been invented yet.

A study of economics reveals that the best time to buy anything is last year.

Remember when a video workout consisted of changing TV channels without owning a remote control?

Notice in paper: "I wish to thank anyone who so kindly assisted in the death of my husband."

The trouble with some people is that they won't put their best foot forward until they're on their last legs.

"This party is very dull," said the rude guest to the hostess. "I think I'll go."
"Please do," was the reply, "That will help some".

Thank goodness for television commercials, they, at least, get us off of our couches.

Sometimes when you're trying to get both ends to meet, somebody moves the ends.

These days a good conversationalist is anyone who can talk louder than the TV and stereo.

You know why they call it take-home pay, don't you? Where else could you afford to go with it?

Honesty is the best policy, but there are few policy holders.

If you approach growing old with a laugh, it's not so frightening. It's simply terrifying.

If we can't believe anything we hear and only half of what we see, then we need to be really careful what we think about.

Q: Why did the baker quit making doughnuts?
A: He was tired of the hole business.

Divorce lawyers tend to think of cars and furniture as 'parting gifts'.

If you watch a game, it's fun. If you play it, it's recreation. If you work at, it's golf.

Girl: One ticket please.
Movie ticket seller: That's the third ticket you've bought in the last five minutes.
Girl: I know but the man inside keeps tearing them up.

Being low man on the totem pole isn't all bad, at least you're on it.

Can there ever be a true friendship between a man and a woman if sexual attraction is totally lacking?

Pessimist: When he has nothing to worry about, he worries about why he has nothing to worry about.

When I was a kid my family was in iron and steel. My mother took in ironing and my dad would steal.

Apartment house walls can be too thin when you're trying to sleep and too thick when you're trying to listen.

The problem with doing something right the first time is that nobody appreciates how difficult it was.

Years ago people lived silently with their frustrations. These days they tell all on talk shows.

Q: Do ants have brains?
A: Of course. How else would they figure out when you're having a picnic?

Automobile manufacturers never will devise a safety device as good as a rearview mirror with a highway trooper in it.

Seasons change. We go from nose blowers to snow blowers.

Q: What do you call a gossiping Eskimo?
A: A blubber mouth.

We once thought that the world was flat, then we thought it was round. Now we know it is crooked.

I don't exercise, but I have been a pallbearer for a lot that did.

Talk used to be cheap. Now, people pay $10 to sit next to you and do it.

One of the hardest things for me to accept is that my worst enemy is somebody's best friend.

He's not a failure. He just started at the bottom and liked it there.

Airline schedules do have their uses, they show you how late the planes are.

The most careful driver is by far the driver of a shiny new car that isn't insured yet.

When a fellow's down, folks want to help him up, until he gets up enough to need taking down a peg or two.

A celebrity is a person who works hard all his life to become well known, then wears dark glasses to avoid being recognized.

We like to think that our weaknesses are inherited, but that our accomplishments are our own ideas.

104

A law of science says you can't put more into a container than it will hold. Designer jeans break that law every day.

In less than 10 years there will be more than 200 million cars on the roads, so if you want to cross the street, you'd better do it now.

Psychoanalysis is a wonderful discovery. It makes quite simple people feel they're complex.

It's easy to identify people who can't count to ten. They're in front of you in the supermarket express lane.

We the willing, led by the unknowing, are doing the impossible for the ungrateful. We have done so much, for so long, with so little, we are now qualified to do anything with nothing. (*I don't know what this means, but it sounded good.*)

Don't worry about avoiding temptation. As you grow older, it will avoid you.

I've never had a problem that was as easy to solve as someone else's.

You can't get rid of a bad temper by losing it.

More people quote William Shakespeare than ever read him.

Dancing is the art of pulling your feet away faster than your partner can step on them.

Why is the person who snores always the first one to fall asleep?

Nowadays you don't really need a car. There are so many people who want to take you for a ride.

Most human beings have an almost infinite capacity for taking things for granted.

If you want support for an idea, try to find someone who thinks the idea is his.

When we use one evil to correct another, we are only perpetuating our troubles.

People ask God why he doesn't do something about the homeless and starving people of the world. Don't they realize that God is asking them the same question?

If you think a seat belt is uncomfortable, have you ever tried a stretcher?

Isn't it odd how a few years can turn 'these trying times' into 'the good old days'?

The only trouble with child psychology is that children don't understand it.

The worst thing about living in a motor home is that there's no place to put anything, except where it belongs.

One of the world's most unsightly packages is a person wrapped up in himself.

Most people admire a good loser, as long as it is somebody else.

The Grand Canyon was created by a Scot who dropped a nickel into a gopher hole.

President and Mrs. Reagan walked by a crowd of photographers toward the helicopter waiting on the White House grounds, a gust of wind blew Nancy's skirt above her waist. The President reached over to try to bring the billowing skirt under control. "Don't bother, honey," Nancy said. "It's your ass they want, not mine."

Parents have to learn to see the best in things, for instance, if your daughter comes home from college with a little bundle in her arms, be glad when it's the laundry.

One afternoon, two mosquitoes were riding on the back of Robinson Crusoe. "I have to go now," said one of the mosquitoes, "But let's meet again on Friday."

Jim and Tammy made so much dough they were called the wonder bakers.

Most folks will accept criticism they think is meant for someone else.

Don't be to timid to ask for help or to proud to accept a gift.

You can tell how big a man is by observing how much it takes to discourage him.

Some of us treat our bodies as if we had a spare in the trunk.

Generous deeds would be repeated more often if more gratitude had been shown for the first ones.

If you wonder what the world is coming to, remember: so did your grandfather.

I always seem to encounter more folks who are concerned about their rights than their obligations.

If there is anything to reincarnation, many of us did not learn much from former lives.

The good thing about dreams is that if they don't come true, you can always dream new ones.

A habit is something you can do without thinking, which is why most of us have so many of them.

The face that over cocktails seemed so sweet
may not look so hot over shredded wheat.

Great occasions for helping others come seldom, but small ones surround us daily.

All women want is hequality.

The great shock of life is learning that people are not perfect; the greater shock is finding out that neither are we.

Many fail as leaders of men because too much of their time is spent as followers, of women.

The reason we don't understand each other is that we expect everyone will be like us.

Television enables you to be entertained in your home by people you wouldn't have in your home.

Woman to a friend: "We're only staying together because of the children. Neither of us wants them."

The people we can't forget are often the ones we don't want to remember.

It is with narrow-minded people as with narrow-necked bottles - the less they have in them, the more noise they make in pouring it out.

Why, when we are so amply supplied with words of praise, do we spend them in such miserly fashion?

107

Of all sad words of tongue or pen, the saddest are these: "But it was guaranteed!"

Man grumbling to friend: "Can't help being depressed. I just realized it's costing me more to insure my car than my life!"

Where do law students study? In the Lie-brary, of course.

Only that traveling is good, reveals to me the value of home and enables me to enjoy it better.

There are two kinds of gratitude: the sudden king we feel for what we take; the larger kind we feel for what we give.

Now there's a movie about a televangelist - it's titled 'The Lust Weekend."

Through the miracle of modern communication we can hear the same news bulletins all day long.

We're usually able to modify our morals enough to justify what we've decided to do.

Our highways aren't safe, our streets aren't safe, our parks aren't safe, but under our arms we've got complete protection.

Talk about the power of advertising - Bumper stickers, signs, and TV commercials are all saying Buy America and the Chinese are doing just that.

What a great country this is. Anybody can have a second house, a second car, a second TV. All it takes is a second job, a second mortgage and a second wind.

When you put down the good things you ought to have done, and leave out the bad ones you did do, that's memoirs.

Wall Street has a lot of people who are really going places. The problem is, one of the places is prison.

Lawyers do everything by the book - the bank book.

Mother to daughter: "Men are all alike. They sweep you off your feet and then hand you the broom."

A great many people seem to end up over the hill without ever having actually climbed it.

You can bet your bottom dollar that a piece of mail that looks like a check isn't.

Whenever somebody says "That's a good question," it usually means you're going to get a lousy answer.

I talked to my plants but they never replied;
then I tried singing and that's when they died.

There are no hard women, only soft men.

Being born beautiful must be cruel, it's like being born rich and getting poorer each year.

A neighbor will stand at your door and chat for twenty minutes because she doesn't have time to come in.

Psychologists say people who watch sports on TV hour after hour are not likely to go crazy, but that doesn't apply to the people they live with.

We mortals realize the value of our blessings only when we have lost them.

Never bet on a sure thing unless you can afford to lose.

Who says they don't have silent prayers in schools? What do you think happens every time they pass out report cards?

When a man tells me he's going to put all his cards on the table, I always look up his sleeve.

Divorce lawyer's ad: "I unlock the lock in wedlock."

A house is built with money, a home with love.

Never mind the things that are as good as new. Let's have some things that are as good as old.

It is fortune, not wisdom that rules man's life.

Two ladies talking - One asks the other one, "What do you do with your panties when you wear them out?"
The other lady said, "I try to find them so that I can wear them home."

One of life's little ironies is that the habits we have to kick are those that give us a kick.

Education has changed a lot since I went to school. In those days you didn't get credit for learning about sex, you got punished,

If you make a mistake, you are a bumbling stupid idiot. If the computer makes a mistake, it's merely a malfunction.

Solitude is a good place to visit, but a poor place to stay.

I'm not sure civilization has done anything for man except to make him run where he used to walk.

We brag about our strengths, but we really love our weaknesses.

Who recalls when folks got along without something if it cost too much?

The fellow who can't figure out what to do with a Sunday afternoon is often the same one who can't wait for retirement.

Man, teaching wife to drive: "Go on green. Stop on red. Take it easy when I turn white."

If you have half a mind to do something, perhaps it would be wise to check with the other half before acting.

People who buy clothes on the installment plan get dressed on time.

What is the best way to talk to a monster? Long distance.

If you are willing to admit you are all wrong when you are all wrong, you are all right.

It has been my experience that folks who have no vices have very few virtues

Truth, like a girdle, is often s-t-r-e-t-c-h-e-d.

Now they're packing sardines in plastic - it's uncanny.

The surest way to avoid getting a bad reputation is to do nothing anybody will remember.

When you shoot the breeze with somebody, remember to let some of the air come from the other person.

Doesn't it seem some days as though other people were put in the world for no other reason than to aggravate you?

The danger is not that our aim is too high and we miss it, but that it is too low and we reach it.

You can tell when people are well informed. Their views are pretty much like your own.

Then somebody says, "I hope you won't mind my telling you this," its a pretty sure thing that you will.

Nothing seems to bring on an emergency as quickly as putting money aside in case of one.

There's nothing wrong with the average person that a good psychologist can't exaggerate.

Some things will never change: Motherly love, the beauties of nature, and the plots of daytime soap operas.

The only normal people are the ones you don't know very well.

A lot of those who offer "expert' advice are experts only at giving advice.

The trouble with learning from experience is that you get the test before the lesson.

The people who have all the luck are those who don't depend on it.

A broken promise is much like a broken teacup; No matter how securely it is mended, it will always remain suspect.

All men are tempted, there is no man that lives that can't be broken down, provided it is the right temptation put in the right spot.

It's not best that we should all think alike; it is difference of opinion that makes horse races.

It seems that every time we graduate from the school of experience, someone comes up with a new course.

The people who turn out best are those people who make the best out of the way things turn out.

There's no lovelier smile than the one of a good fortune.

Nothing is wonderful when you get use to it.

Giant oak trees started out as little nuts that stood their ground.

Don't wait until you feel better to do good; do good and you'll begin to feel better.

Success: getting what you want
Happiness: liking what you get.

The wise know that the best way to get even is to get ahead.

Real patience is the ability to count down before blasting off.

A pessimist is a person who is seasick during the entire voyage of life.

Worry often gives a small thing a big shadow.

Showing the latest pictures of your kids to your co-workers gives a whole new meaning to the term 'low interest rates'.

The worst thing about fishing is, when you don't catch any and you can't blame a computer.

Many people waste their time trying to see through one another instead of trying to see one another through.

A dentist and a carpenter got married, but it didn't work out. They kept fighting tooth and nail.

The average person looks on sacrifice the way we look on a lightning bolt. It's fine, providing it doesn't come too close to home.

We act as though comfort and luxury were the chief requirements of life, when all that we need to make us really happy is something to be enthusiastic about.

Most of us are too critical of ourselves, but not critical enough to make changes.

Those who concern themselves with the happiness of others usually result in making their neighbors miserable.

Most human beings have an almost infinite capacity for taking things for granted.

You've got spunk. I hate spunk.

What counts is necessarily the size of the dog in the fight - it's the size of the fight in the dog.

I keep my ideals, because in spite of everything, I still believe that people are really good at heart.

Better than making a name for oneself is making a life for others.

Nothing is as stressful as trying to be a person different from who you are.

You'll never stumble on anything while sitting down.

A person who is never wrong has guessed right more than once.

Courage and perseverance often cause difficulties to disappear.

A person who makes no mistakes usually does not make anything.

Courage is fear that has said its prayers.

We never get dizzy from doing good turns.

I'd kill for a Nobel Peace Prize.

A conscience is what hurts when all your other parts feel so good.

How can you tell when you're out of invisible ink?

Depression is merely anger without enthusiasm.

Ok. So what's the speed of dark?

A clear conscience is usually the sign of a bad memory.

If everything seems to be going well, you have obviously overlooked something.

The idealist is incorrigible; if he is thrown out of his heaven, he makes an ideal of his hell.

I keep my ideals, because in spite of everything, I still believe that people are really good at heart.

We can't all be heroes; someone has to sit on the curb and clap as they go by.

No wishbone ever took the place of a backbone.

It's a consolation to know that no one can make a fool out of you but yourself.

People who look for the easy way out seem to have trouble finding an exit.

If you promise not to repeat something, does that mean you can tell it only once?

An organ grinder's tune may sound like Mozart, but it's by handle.

Anger is a dark room where negatives are developed.

You can either agree with me or be wrong.

When pessimists think they're taking a chance, optimists feel they're grasping a great opportunity.

Character is a diamond that scratches every stone.

Tell me, I'll forget. Show me, I may remember, but involve me, and I'll understand.

Flexible people never get bent out of shape.

Do not be afraid of dreaming the seemingly impossible if you want the seemingly impossible to become a reality.

I am a great believer in luck and the harder I work, the more I have of it.

I am not trying to be difficult, it just comes naturally.

Every great idea I have gets me in trouble.

Elephants and grandchildren never forget.

The important things about your lot in life is whether you use it for parking or building.

Nonsense is good only because common sense is so limited.

The only person who gets anywhere playing both ends against the middle is an accordion player.

A pessimist is seldom disappointed.

I saw a woman wearing a sweatshirt with "Guess" on it. So I said "Implants?" She hit me.

Why do we choose from just two people to run for President and over fifty for Miss America?

When all else fails, read the instructions.

A cynic is someone who knows the price of everything and the value of nothing.

Don't argue with an idiot; people watching may not be able to tell the difference.

Ever since Eve gave Adam the apple, there has been a misunderstanding between the sexes about gifts.

Angels can fly because they take themselves lightly.

When do cows to sleep? When it's 'pasture' bedtime.

A man is as big as the things that make him angry.

It's usually easier to do right than to explain why you did wrong.

You make a living by what you get, you make a life by what you give.

A prune is just a plum that's over the hill.

To test your memory, try to remember what you worried about last week.

If at first you don't succeed, get ready to hear lots of advice.

You don't need a search warrant when looking for trouble.

An argument is a head-on collision of two trains of thought.

Many think nothing needs reforming as much as other people's habits.

When it's hardest to pray is when you should pray the hardest.

If your Christmas gift list fits on a self-stick note, you may need to get out more.

If at first you don't succeed, you are probably about revenge.

Silence should never be broken unless it can be improved on.

Why is it that our children can't read a Bible in school, but they can in prison?

Bumper sticker of the year: "If you can read this, thank a teacher, and since it's in English, thank a soldier."

If you think you never make a mistake, you might be mistaken.

I'm not perfect, but so close it scares me.

Don't look back, somebody may be gaining on you.

The trouble with being a good sport is that you have to lose to prove it.

With two eyes and one mouth, we're made to speak about half of what we see.

A loose tongue can get you into tight places.

An expert is one who tells you more about something than you want to know.

Mistletoe may be bad for trees, but it seems to be fun twos.

Don't pet your pet peeve too much.

I may be left handed, but I'm always right.

Never to bed mad - stay up and plot your revenge.

Whenever things sound easy, it turns out there is one part you didn't hear.

Nothing that makes a memory is wasteful.

The only way to fight a cold is blow by blow.

A bad habit is like a soft chair—easy to get into, but hard to get out of.

There is something more important than IQ – it's "I will."

At my age some times I stop to think and forget to start again.

I could do the work of two men, but I would have to slow down.

Forget the list of things to do, it's easier to list things already done.

If your mind wanders don't worry it may be too weak to go very far. It takes a big person to refrain from small remarks.

The only thing that gets thicker as it spreads is a rumor.

Why is it that opportunity knocks only once, but temptation never stops?

To get on in life, get up each time you get down.

Blessed are those who give without remembering and receive without forgetting.

Stability is not immobility.

What did the left sock say to his mate? I think we got off on the wrong foot.

The beaten path is the safest, but the traffic is terrible.

I'm older than dirt and have more scars than Frankenstein, but I've learned a few things on the way.

The can-do spirit is the fuel that makes things go.

Creativity is a habit, and the best creativity is a result of good work habits.

I will love the light for its shows me the way, yet I will endure the darkness for it shows me the stars.

Some people find that the most difficult instrument to learn to play is second fiddle.

The measure of real character is what a person would do, knowing he or she never would be found out.

If you feel you have no faults, that makes another one.

Encouragement and kindness are the best of gifts.

It is by working that a person finds out what he or she is able to do.

Many eyes go through the meadow, but few see all the flowers in it.

A thousand words will not leave as deep an impression as one deed.

Modesty is the only sure bait when you angle for praise.

About the only time losing is more fun than winning is when you're fighting temptation.

What does it mean when you find a bear with a wet nose? It means you're to close to the bear.

Honk if you like our quiet little town.

Sex and golf are the two things you can enjoy even if you're not good at them.

Our first stop as new recruits was the barber shop. He asked, "Want to keep your sideburns?" "Yes that would be great," I said. "Okay, I'll get you a bag to put them in.

What happens in swimwear stays in swimwear.

Cooperation is doing with a smile what you have to do anyway.

An apology is a good way to have the last word.

The bird of paradise alights only upon the hand that does grasp.

Clothiers give good customers on-the-cuff treatment.

In each of us there is a little of all of us.

Talkative tailors yarn on till the end of twine.

Fool me once, shame on you; fool me twice shame on me.

Just when you think you've graduated from the school of experience, someone thinks up a new course.

The most flammable kind of wood is the chip on the shoulder.

What happens when you cross a lollipop with a rabbit? A sucker's born every minute.

Why did the football coach to the bank? To get his quarterback.

I want to feel your sweet embrace, but don't take that paper bag off your face.

The thing I hate about an argument is that it always interrupts a discussion.

It's not the altitude it's the attitude.

Librarians have to go by the book.

Excellence is to do a common thing in an uncommon way.

Tact is the knack of making a point without making an enemy.

Having to explain it means you probably shouldn't have said it.

It's like magic, when you live by yourself, all of your annoying habits are gone.

Beauty is not with the face; beauty is a light in the heart.

Nuttier than a squirrel's breakfast.

NAMEN - BLAMEN - SHAMEN - FRAMEN - Attorney $ At Law.

I can resist anything but temptation; my will is strong, but my won't is weak.

The difference between news and gossip is whether you hear it or tell it.

Don't admire strong silent types too soon; they may merely be dumb.

There are two reasons for distrusting people. We do not know them, and we do know them.

Put yourself in his shoes.

You have to be good to the cow to get the calf.

Make the best of every situation, good or bad.

Guard what you say to anyone, as your words may be the last they'll hear.

It's nice to generate some sunshine in the world whenever and wherever you can.

Try and leave the world a little better for your having been there.

It's nice to clean up Main Street, but you have to clean down the alleys, too.

There's a place for everything, so keep everything in its place.

A bad penny will always return.

When you move if you take a good neighbor with you, you'll have a good neighbor.

A favor done, with a favor expected in return, is not a favor to begin with.

Repeat only the good, don't tell tales out of school.

Where there's smoke, someone has at least thought of building a fire.

Beautiful fantasies float on a sea of reality - the problem is to prevent leaks.

It is true that ultra-conservatives miss a lot, but don't be so open minded that your brains fall out.

It is much easier to be critical than to be correct.

People who cannot lead and refuse to follow make a dandy roadblock. They impede progress and are hard on the nerves.

My specialty is being right when other people are wrong.

Quarrels would not last long if the fault was only on one side.

I don't care anything about reasons, but I know what I like.

Some folk want their luck buttered too.

If he has no other burden, he'll take up a load of stones.

One often contradicts an opinion when it is really only the tone in which it has been presented that is unsympathetic.

Follow-through builds trust.

If at first you do not succeed, sky diving is not for you.

Many troubles would burn to ashes and blow away if we did not refuel them with flames of hatred.

Language is not the only means of communication; there's smiling, touching, laughing - the list is long.

Some people will do anything to get attention, but deserve it.

You can only peel one potato at a time.

Our distrust justifies the deceit of others.

Hanging onto resentments is letting someone you despise live rent-free in your head.

The man who claims he is boss in his own home will probably lie about other things, too.

A clean glove often hides a dirty hand.

If we examine well the diverse effects of boredom, we shall find that it causes us to neglect more duties than does the interest.

It takes two to quarrel; it takes the same two to reconcile.

To pursue the absolute impossible is madness.

Teacher:. "If say, I have went out, why is that incorrect?
Pupil: "Because you ain't went out, yet."

Pride is an arch seducer of reason.

Look upon those around you with understanding than with criticism.

Don't let the world around you squeeze you into its mold; look for the best, and become it.

To lighten up a dreary day, look through clouds with a colored glass.

We are not "everybody", and we are proud to be different.

There's no pot so crooked that you can't find a lid to fit it.

You wrote the letter and got it off your chest. Now don't send it.

You forgot? Then next time you better for-think.

Everything that happens is for the best.

There are 869 different forms of lying, but only one of them has been squarely forbidden. Thou shalt not bear false witness against thy neighbor.

Often, the surest way to convey misinformation is to tell the strict truth.

SATAN (impatiently) to new-comer: The trouble with you Chicago people is that you think you are the best people down here; whereas you are merely the most numerous.

In the first place God made idiots. This was for practice. Then He made School Boards.

There are no people who are quite so vulgar as the over-refined ones.

Let us be thankful for the fools. But for them the rest of us could not succeed.

121

The man with a new idea is a "crank" until the idea succeeds.

Let us be thankful to Adam our benefactor. He cut us out of the "Blessing" of idleness and won for us the "curse" of labor.

Let us not be too particular. It is better to have old secondhand diamonds than none at all.

There are several good protections against temptations, but the surest is cowardice.

Names are not always what they seem. The common Welsh name Bzjxxllwep is pronounced Jackson. -

Truth is the most valuable thing we have. Let us economize it.

Noise proves nothing. Often a hen who has merely laid an egg cackles as if she had lain an asteroid.

As shy as a newspaper is when referring to its own merits.

A dozen direct censures are easier to bear than one morganatic compliment.

We often give our enemies the means for our own destruction.

The surest sign there is intelligent life on other planets is that no one has ever tried to get in touch with us.

One size does not fit all. Re: "One man's meat is another man's poison."

It isn't important to come out on top; what matters most is to be the one who comes out alive.

The shortest distance between two points is in one ear and out the other.

A man may have no bad habits and have worse.

It is your human environment that makes climate.

The English are mentioned in the Bible: Blessed are the meek, for they shall inherit the earth.

It is easier to stay out than to get out.

Pity is for the living, envy is for the dead.

Confidence is the feeling you have before you really understand the problem.

Nothing is quite so annoying as to have someone go right on talking when you're interrupting.

Faith is believing what you know isn't so.

Q: How is a convict like a tuna?
A: Both struggle to get off the hook, but wind up in the can.

Boy! I feel so good this morning 'I think I'll call in sick.

Wishing and hoping and praying are poor substitutes for action.

Suspicion is what drives you to find out something you'd rather not know.

Don't bend over backwards to please anybody, unless you're sure there will be somebody there to catch you when you fall.

Few things are harder to put up with than a good example.

Q: How do you fix a broken watermelon?
A: With a watermelon patch

The person who looks up to God rarely looks down on people.

Every year it takes less time to fly around the world and more time to drive to work.

Shh! "And has your baby learned to talk yet?
"Oh, yes, we're teaching him to keep quiet now."

Another unsolved mystery is why people who snore always' fall asleep first.

If to err is human, then weathermen must be a lot more human than most.

The squeaking wheel may get the grease, or it may be the first to be replaced.

To ignore an insult is the true test of moral courage.

Having fun is a lot like life Insurance. The older you get, the more it costs.

Q: What do you call a skeleton in a closet?
A: Last year's hide-and-sick champion.

Nothing in fine print is ever good news.

Highways are full of careless drivers who are always too close in front of you.

Where I come from, a cultured person is one that doesn't drink red wine from a jar.

The bigger stick you swing, the less time you actually have to hit someone with it.

A cynic is a pessimist with experience.

If you are trying to carry too many items, you will only drop the most breakable one.

It is a victory if we did better than we thought we could.

Q: Why did the stoplight turn red?
A: You would too if you had to change in the middle of the Street.

The one redeeming feature of being wrong is the joy it brings to others.

Remember when a hard drive was an arduous car trip, and not a computer part?

Any truly great venture has some potential for disaster.

If it goes without saying, then don't say it.

The person who rocks the boat is seldom the one pulling the oars.

Ever notice when someone says, "Do you want my honest opinion?' It's always a negative one?

Those proud of keeping an orderly desk never know the thrill of finding something they thought was irretrievably lost.

First monster: Why did you eat those tightrope walkers?
Second monster: I like a well-balanced diet.

Be true to your teeth or they will be false to you.

I have a knee problem - my wife caught my secretary on it.

The guy who talks his head off isn't loosing much.

You have to grow up to have troubles.

A new broom sweeps clean, but the old brush knows the corners.

It takes less time to do a thing right than it does to explain why you did it wrong.

The tongue weighs practically nothing, but so few people are able to hold it.

Confusions might help a man's conscience, but not his reputation.

A small town is a place where there's no place to go where you shouldn't.

The best thing for gray hair is respect.

Light travels faster than sound, which explains why some people appear bright until they start talking.

Ambition is when you want to be somebody. Envy is when you want to be somebody else.

Nobody likes a liar unless it's the bathroom scale.

Be on the level and you are not likely to go downhill.

Man: How did you come to fall in the lake, little boy?
Boy: I didn't come to fall in the lake mister, I came to fish.

A tourist is a person who travels to find things that are different, and then complains when they are.

The reason driving a car was more fun in the old days is because the crank was in front of the engine.

Q: How many successful jumps must a paratrooper make before he graduates?
A: All of them.

Some people change their ways when they see the light. Others change only when they feel the heat.

Jim: "Gosh I need $20 and I don't know where to get it."
Tom: "I'm sure glad of that. I was afraid you thought you could get it from me!"

Most people are willing to take the Sermon on the Mount as a flag to sail under, but few will use it as a rudder by which to steer.

Ever notice that people never say 'It's only a game' when they are winning.

Teachers are people who used to like children.

Prayer is not asking for what we lack, but giving thanks for what we have.

Most people who sing their own praises can't carry a tune.

He's so conceited; he found his better half in the mirror.

Complacency is the refuge of those who have lost the dream.

When you speak before thinking, you jump to confusion.

A Texan was visiting Niagara Falls with a friend from New York. "I'll bet you don't have anything like this in Texas", the New Yorker said.
"No", admitted the Texan, "but we have plumbers who could fix it!

The difference between looking good and good looking is 20 years and 20 pounds.

He that can't endure the bad will not live to see the good.

The good old days were when a rush hour only lasted an hour.

The more you talk about your troubles the harder it is to find somebody who'll listen.

If you remember "FLAT FOOT FLOOGIE WITH A FLOY, FLOY" what right do you have to be critical of today's music?

Don't you wish all those people trying to find themselves would get lost?

He who foresees calamities suffers them twice over.

The only dumb question is the one you should have asked and didn't.

That extra mile is never crowded.

Did you hear about the cannibal who had a him on rye?

There's no deed so foul but what some lawyer will call its perpetrator a fine, decent, upstanding citizen.

Give most freeway drivers an inch and they will switch lanes.

When a person sits quietly just thinking about things, chances are the TV set is out of order.

Most people miss their calling because they can't hear it over their complaining.

The shortest distance between two points is no longer a straight line. It's a remote control unit.

The greatest truths are the simplest, and so are the greatest men.

One can acquire everything in solitude - except character.

Did you ever wonder what language truck drivers are using now that everyone is using theirs?

Brooding over troubles is a good way to make them hatch.

Lets be fair about this. There's a very good reason for lawyers. Think how boring the world would be if everything was as simple as it really is.

Troubles are like weeds in a garden, we should try to remove them, but if we concentrate only on them, we miss the good things.

The difference between nosiness and advice is whether you pay for it.

One thing about paying compliments: They don't cost more every year.

The difference between gossip and news depends on whether you are hearing it or telling it.

Of course there's a devil. Who do you think tickles your nose as soon as your arms are full of packages?

SIGN OUTSIDE A BEAUTY SHOP: We will curl up and dye for you.

A man is not religious because of what he believes, but because he lives what he believes.

Some televangelists seem mote interested in the fleece than in the flock.

Fears of expressing ourselves makes us prisoners of our thoughts.

Prayer begins where human capacity ends.

People are like envelopes: those stamped 'important' seldom are.

Ever notice that people never tell you nice things 'for your own good'?

Some troubles come from wanting to have our own way; others come from being allowed to have it.

If there is intelligent life on other planets, they are at least intelligent enough to stay away from us.

Would you like to hear the story about Dolly Parton's tight sweater? It's an outstanding yarn.

We are all handicapped people; it's just that the majority of us have handicaps which don't show.

Football is a game in which 22 big, strong men run around like crazy for two hours while 50,000 people who really need the exercise watch them.

I don't understand it. TV evangelists tell us how sinful, immoral and deceitful we are then ask us to send them money.

Having good manners is what keeps you from correcting folks with bad manners.

Some people have lousy memories, they never forget anything.

Those who spend today boasting about the wonderful things they will do tomorrow probably spent yesterday doing the same things.

It matters little what else in life you earn if you do not earn love. Reprove a friend in secret, but praise him before others.

We understand death for the first time when he puts his hand upon one whom we love.

We see with our eyes. We hear with our ears. We judge with our emotions.

Two things more difficult than work are looking for it and trying to avoid it.

Those breakfast food companies could sell 25 percent more cereal than they're selling right now - fill the boxes!

Mechanic to customer; "I'm afraid you have more of a problem than I anticipated. Your battery needs a new car.

Teach me to be right instead of wrong, and help me to live with others when I am right.

The biggest fault some people have is always finding fault in others.

The eyes believe themselves; the ears believe other people.

The only thing most of us are willing to give until it hurts is criticism.

To comprehend what the human mind is capable of, imagine the planet earth void of all that has been created by the human mind!

San Francisco is like granola! Take away the fruits and the nuts, and all you have left are the flakes.

When somebody tells you that something defies description, you can be pretty sure he's going to have a go at it anyway.

A lot of the new TV shows have happy endings – you are glad when they are over.

When a man is wrong, and won't admit it, he always gets angry.

Nobody likes a crooked lawyer until he needs one.

A lot of people who join groups to clean up the environment could start by cleaning out their own garages.

Show me a guy who left his heart in San Francisco and I'll show you a guy with a hole in his chest.

The Lord created the world in six days. On the seventh day he rested. On the eighth he started to answer complaints.

The reason we don't learn from the mistakes of others is that we are to busy making our own.

You can usually persuade folks to agree pretty well about anything that doesn't concern them.

Beauty sleep does not beauty make: Think how we look when we first awake

Of course talk is cheap: The supply always exceeds the demand.

If there is no hell, a good many preachers are obtaining money under false pretenses.

Bert's Observations

Overheard: "After a long vacation in Europe, they returned home, brag and baggage.'

Whenever I open a present
My mental gyrations are swift:
Whether to keep it, return it
or recycle it as a gift.

To speak ill of others is a dishonest way of praising ourselves.

The minute a man is convinced that he is interesting, he isn't.

It's amazing how many drivers learn about the law by accident.

Love

Love

If your heart is full of love, you always have something to give.

Love can be divided endlessly and still not diminish.

When love and skill work together expect a masterpiece.

We have a lot in common. I love you and you love me.

A life without love is like a year without summer.

There are spaces between our fingers so that another person's fingers can fill them in.

A candle loses none of its light by lighting another candle.

Don't look for love; give love - and you will find love looking for you.

To many people believe in loss of love at first slight.

If the world seems cold to you, kindle caring fires to warm it.

Warm hearts, not hot heads maintain the right temperature at home.

LOVE is the most beautiful discovery of all. One that is meant to be shared by two.

Choose your life's mate carefully, from this one decision will come 90 percent of all your happiness or misery.

Love is when the other person's happiness is more important than your own.

Once you have learned to love, you have learned to live.

If at first you don't succeed - try a little ardor.

If you want to find love, instead of looking for ways to attract it, lose all that's in you that repulses it.

Love is a many - mended thing.

We can do without being loved, but we can not afford to live without love.

The first duty of love is to listen.

In living, have compassion, let loving he your aim. The crying of your enemy and your brother sound the same.

If you wish to he loved, show more of your faults than your virtues.

To love is to place our happiness in the happiness of another.

It is not love we should have painted as blind, but self love.

The greatest weakness of most humans is their hesitancy to tell others how much they love them while they're still alive.

Love is life. Everything else either adds to or detracts from it.

One cannot love what he cannot respect, whether it be himself or another.

You can try to teach people what love is by loving them, but they will never know what love is until they love someone.

People bemoan the fact that love doesn't last; neither does an ice cream cone, but it's delicious while it does.

It isn't how much one does for another that counts, but how much love one does it with.

Love is like life insurance, the older you get, the more it costs.

You cannot love a thing without wanting to fight for it.

If you're trying to learn to love, start with something easy, like children.

To want to be with someone all the time is infatuation.
To have to be with someone all the time is obsession.
To feel you are with someone all the time whether you are or not is love.

If you want to be loved, you have to be worth loving.

Love is a condition of the mind at a time when the mind is out of condition.

A heart is judged not by how much you love, but by how much you are loved by others.

No love is more inspiring than that of the long-married couple, where he still considers a joy to behold and she still considers it a joy to be held.

Love

Those who love deeply never grow old; they may die of old age, but they die young.

Love is blind; it actually sees more, but is willing to see less.

Real love begins when nothing is expected in return.

LOVE IS....
Letting him think he thought of it first.
Letting him read the newspaper first.
Wearing the tie she bought for your birthday.
Biting your tongue when she left your new spade out in the rain.
Praying together.
Buckling up every time you drive.
Shaving off your mustache if she doesn't like it.
That first kiss in the morning.
Letting him have the last sip of wine.
Spending every spare minute together.

Only love can be divided endlessly and still not diminish.

True love doesn't consist of holding hands - it consists of holding hearts.

Some things are loved because they are valuable, others because they are loved.

Love lures people, both the ones who give it and the ones who receive it.

Real love begins when nothing is expected in return.

Love doesn't make the world go round: It's what makes the ride worthwhile.

Everybody needs a hug - it changes your metabolism.

Age does not protect you from love, but love, to some extent, protects you from age.

Where there is love there is life.

I believe that unarmed truth and unconditional love will have the final word in reality.

Love should be cherished, not wasted.

The heart that loves is always young.

Love is free, but it requires a lifetime of dedication.

Hatred spews from the mouths of the unloved.

Love must be re-grown from time-to-time.

Thinking of you helps me see the beauty of each day.

You can give without loving, but you can't love without giving.

It's the nature of love to work in a thousand different ways.

On a game show, a contestant was asked to name a great time saver. The reply, "Love at first sight."

No one love is adequate for life; our lives are given color by the many people we love.

Time may heal all wounds, but love will do it quicker.

Of course I remember my first love, it was ice cream.

Love begins when the needs of someone else become more important than your own.

Love that has nothing but beauty to keep it in good health is short lived.

If you can't love a person for what he is, love him for what you can help him become.

Those who have learned to love most have learned to forgive most.

Self-love is the only enduring passion.

The time we waste trying to find out what life is all about could be spent loving someone and finding out.

Love is wanting life's best for another, even if it does not include you.

If you can't love people, find something about them to like, when they like you for it, you will love them.

We too often love things and use people, when we should be using things and loving people.

Love

Where there is great love, there are always miracles.

Love never looks to see what it is going to get in return.

Loving is easy. It's the living together that's so damned hard.

There is no shame in crying, only in not feeling.

To love and be loved is to feel the sun from both sides.

At the touch of love, everyone becomes a poet.

Love me when I least deserve it, because that's when I really need it.

Love has nothing to do with what you're expecting to get - only with what you are expecting to give - which is everything.

Love is not lost if you give it away.

If you have not loved, you have not lived.

In labors of love, every day is payday.

Time endears but cannot fade, the memories that love has made.

I find as I grow older that I love those most whom I loved first.

Laughter

Laughter

Laugh lines should be the guidelines for wrinkle lines.

Learn to laugh at yourself—you'll have a life long source of amusement.

I left her laughing; the sound was like hen having hiccups.

Laughter is medicine to weary bones.

One of the best things a person can have up his sleeve is a funny bone.

The sound of laughter carries further than the sound of weeping.

Everyone can afford to give away a smile.

It is nice that we never have to teach children when and how to laugh.

By nothing do men show their character more than by the things they laugh at.

Troubles scurry when laughter shows its face.

Make it a point to indulge in at least one hearty laugh every day. If nothing funnier comes along, laugh at yourself.

True life lies in laughter, love, and work.

If you can't laugh at your own mistakes, you have no right to laugh at another's.

A smile is contagious; be a carrier.

Two things are important in my life, sex and laughs. Unfortunately, I get them at the same time.

Laughter comes naturally to children. Hate must be taught.

When you are very busy, don't let humor become one of the things you think you can do without.

We should use smiles often. The Lord made them especially for human beings.

I have often noticed that a kindly placed good humor is the companion of longevity and I suspect, frequently the leading cause of it.

Gravity keeps us down to earth; levity prevents us from becoming mired in the ruts of everyday living.

A sense of humor is a shock absorber on the road of life.

The young man who has not wept is a savage, and the older man who will not laugh is a fool.

Always laugh when you can, it is cheap medicine.

If taking vitamins doesn't keep you healthy enough, try more laughter.

The most wasted of all days is that on which one has not laughed.

A good laugh is sunshine in the house.

If you are too busy to laugh, you're too busy PERIOD.

If a wife laughs at a man's joke, it means that either he has a good joke or a good wife.

Most smiles are started by another smile.

If there's one thing I know, it's God does love a good joke.

Laugh and you'll live without Medicare until you're one hundred.

A smile is a passport that will take you anywhere you want to go.

Once you have them by the funny bone, their hearts and minds will follow.

If you don't learn to laugh at troubles, you won't have anything to laugh at when you're old.

Laugh it off your mother had to.

Laughter makes your whole body feel good.

Smile and the world smiles with you, kick and you kick alone. For a friendly grin will let you in, where a kicker is never known.

The trouble with lawyer jokes is lawyers don't think they're funny, and nobody else thinks they're jokes.

Laughter

Laughter is the best medicine - and the cheapest.

A sense of humor is the ability to laugh at your own jokes if your wife tells them.

No day is complete until you hear the laughter of a child.

If you lose your power to laugh, you lose your power to think.

If laughter really was the best medicine, doctors would figure out a way to charge for it.

We don't cease laughing because we have grown old: We grow old because we cease laughing.

Women laugh at men's jokes, not because the jokes are clever, but because the women are.

Leadership

Leadership

The person who knows how will always have a job, but the person who knows why, will be his boss.

The world was made by many men, but shaped by few. The important thing is to be one of those few.

Courage is contagious. When a brave person takes a stand, the spines of others are stiffened.

A leader knows what's best to do; a manager knows merely how best to do it.

No man can think clearly when his fists are clenched.

The difference between ordinary and extraordinary is the extra you put in the latter.

Do not follow where the path may lead. Go instead where there is no path and leave a trail.

Never underestimate your power to change yourself: Never overestimate your power to change others.

The ultimate test of management is performance.

The sign of a good manager is his ability to give and take negative feedback.

The ultimate test of management is performance.

The worst mistake a boss can make is not to say "well done".

The person who knows how will always have a job, but the person who knows why will be his boss.

Our character is what we do when we think no one is looking.

The very essence of leadership is that you have a vision. You can't blow an uncertain trumpet.

A leader knows what's best to do; a manager knows merely how best to do it.

Nothing unmasks a man like his use of power.

Your legacy should be that you made it better than it was when you got it.

Tell me, and I'll forget. Show me and I may not remember, involve me and I'll understand.

The very essence of leadership is that you have a vision. You can't blow an uncertain trumpet.

A leader knows what's best to do; a manager knows merely how best to do it.

It is important for our leaders to know what we stand for, but it is more important for than to know what we won't stand for.

He who is too important for small tasks is too small for important ones.

The person who knows how will always have a job. The person who knows why, will always he his boss.

He who thinks himself good for everything is often good for nothing.

If you are all wrapped in yourself, you are overdressed.

The price of authority is responsibility.

Anyone can be at the helm when the sea is calm.

Being powerful is like being a lady. If you have to tell people you are, you aren't.

There is a time to let things happen and a time to make things happen.

It's nice to be important, and it's more important to be nice.

Character may be manifested in the great moments, but it is made in the small ones.

The feeling of importance should spring from living importantly.

Man will do many things to get himself loved, he will do all things to get himself envied.

Fame is the perfume of heroic deeds.

Nothing is so strong as tenderness and nothing so gentle as real strength.

Leadership

The ultimate measure of a man is not where he stands in moments of comfort and convenience, but where he stands at times of challenge and controversy.

There is not rest for a messenger till the message is delivered. To ability to accept responsibility is the measure of the man.

The best way to become an overnight success is to work at it for years.

Create your own opportunities by acting the part of the position you desire.

Anybody who thinks there's plenty of room at the top has a lot to learn about pyramids.

Leadership is the ability to get men to do what they don't want to do and like it.

True fame is when you dominate the conversation - after you have left the room.

Compromise is the art of cutting a cake so that everybody believes he or she got the biggest piece.

To be able to lead others, a man must be willing to go forward alone.

Those who are willing to face the music, even when it means a reprimand, are those most likely to eventually lead the band.

What people say behind your back is your standing in the community.

The smartest person in a business is the one who has hired people who are smarter.

Marriage and Family

Marriage and Family

All that I am or ever hope to be I owe to my angel mother.

A wedding is where two people agree to become one; Marriage is the process of deciding which one.

Kids who are as good as gold often go off the gold standard.

Courting hasn't changed much in 2,000 years; ancient Greek women used to sit around all evening and listen to a lyre, too.

Some people think it is holding on that makes one strong—sometimes it's letting go.

Marriage has three rings - The-engagement ring, the wedding ring, and the suffering.

If marriages are made in heaven, they have to be tested here on earth.

Marriage is like a sandwich - the more you add to it, the better it becomes.

Babies are such a nice way to start people.

Many a man falls in love with a dimple and makes the mistake of marrying the whole girl

Children are paparazzi. They take your picture when you don't want them to.

There is no such thing as a non-working mother.

More important than the kind of house you live in is what kind of you is living in the house.

Fatherhood is pretending the present you love most is soap-on-a rope.

Keep your eyes wide open before marriage, half shut afterwards.

When a woman lowers her voice, she wants something. If she raises it, it's a sign that she didn't get it.

One of the most satisfying things in life for parents is seeing their children have teenagers of their own.

The dread of loneliness is greater than the fear of bondage, so we got married.

The only thing so simple a child can operate it, is a grandparent.

Advice for a tranquil marriage: Try to overlook more and oversee less.

A mother takes 20 years to make a man of her boy, and another woman makes a fool of him in 20 minutes.

Every girl needs a small brother to take the conceit out of her.

Many children are expected to learn good manners without seeing any. Intuition isn't scientific, but it's the best of all lie detectors,

Spring housecleaning is about as much fun as hugging a cactus.

Hundred-year old entered college in 1925 gets degree. Claims he had to graduate now because his Dad was tired of paying tuition.

I would rather make my name than inherit it.

Marriage is like a cafeteria. You pick out something that looks good and pay for it down the line.

A house is a place to store furniture. A home is a place to store memories.

Happiness is when your 16-year-old fails the driving test and you know you have a car for another month.

One too many - He paid for bigamy, it stuck in his craw.
The price of polygamy? Two mothers-in-law.

Quite often a wife can be a pearl. It's the mother-of-pearl that makes all the trouble.

Some people have difficulty picking a name for their baby; others have wealthy relatives.

A woman is a person who will spend $25.00 on a beautiful slip and then be annoyed if it shows.

One thing about being married - your mistakes never go unnoticed.

A mother understands what a child doesn't.

When a man steals your wife, there is no better revenge than to let him keep her.

A good wife always forgives her husband when she's wrong.

My kid is forgetful. Last semester be had an open-book final in college, and he forgot his book. This semester they gave him a take-home test and he forgot where he lived.

Parents with kids and only one bathroom can easily understand those foreign wars over territory.

My brother-in-law is just not very bright. He lost his job as an inspector at the M&M factory. He kept throwing away the W's.

Remember when "How many times does a girl get married?" Was a rhetorical question?

The weather and children run true to form: You can expect a lull before the storm.

Bigamy is when you have one wife too many; monogamy is the same thing.

Driving school instructor to a student behind the wheel: "You still have few minutes of your lesson left. Shall I show you how to fill out the accident forms?"

Raising teenagers is like trying to nail Jello to a tree.

Live so that when your children think of fairness and integrity, they will think of you.

Parents lend children their experience and a vicarious memory; children endow their parents with a vicarious immortality.

The world doesn't hear what a father says to his children, but posterity

Heredity is the thing a child gets from the other side of the family.

We often wish we knew as much today as we thought we knew when we were 17.

Some men and women marry for love, some for money, and many for a short time.

Marriage is a feast where the grace is sometimes better than the dinner.

Those who say "you can't take it with you" would really flip if they ever saw our car packed for a vacation trip.

Loving is easy. It's the living together that's so damned hard!

Teenager, explaining the custom or a dowry: "It's like a rebate on a car that they couldn't get rid of otherwise."

A good example of minority rule is when there is a baby in the house.

Advice to youth: Choose to the best you can be; follow the lead of those who succeed.

When children have it made, they sometimes don't learn how to make it.

Marrying an old bachelor is like buying second hand furniture.

Sooner or later every teenager gets what is coming to him; he grows up and becomes a parent too.

The reason that bigamy is against the law is probably because you cannot serve two masters at one time.

Blessed events: The arrival of a baby and a departure of a mother-in-law.

Your legacy should be that you made it better than it was when you got it.

Why waste money looking up your family tree? Just go into politics and your opponents will do it for you.

If the woman wears the pants in the family - her husband's mistress will wear the diamonds.

I am a firm believer in getting married early in the morning. That way, if it doesn't work out you haven't wasted a whole day.

Children have never been very good at listening to their elders, but they never failed to imitate them.

Kids are too young to have to go through adolescence.

The real menace in dealing with a five—year old is that in no time at all you begin to sound like a five year old.

Our tastes change as we mature. Little girls like painted dolls; little boys like soldiers. When they grow up, girls like the soldiers and the boys go for the dolls.

One father can support 12 children, but 12 children cannot support one father.

Sign in a store window: "Bath Towels for the Whole Damp Family."

He took misfortune like a man, he blamed it on his wife.

A fellow gets married due to lack of judgment, divorced due to a lack of patience, and remarried due to lack of memory.

Never close your lips to those to whom you have opened your heart.

If at first you don't succeed, do it the way your wife told you.

Considering the family tree, it's not how high it reaches, but rather, it's how will the nuts be hidden.

The best way to remember an anniversary is to forget one.

One of the hardest things to teach kids about money matters is that it does.

A splendid woman is usually the daughter of her father, just as strong men have noble mothers.

He got new golf clubs for my wife. Gee I wish I could make a trade like that.

Marriage is a lot like living in an earthquake zone. You never know when some little fault will shake the whole house.

A clean house is the sign of a wasted life.

Your marriage is in trouble when your wife suggests you sleep in separate time zones.

A mother-in-law and a daughter-in-law in one house are like two cats in a bag.

Babies may not he able to lift much, but they're strong enough to hold most marriages together.

Hussein's mother should have thrown him away and kept the stork.

A happy marriage is zone in which a man kisses his wife at the door when he leaves in the morning as well as when be returns in the afternoon.

Apron, heart, purse, and harp are the four strongest strings in a man's life.

A boy has two jobs. One is just being a boy. The other is growing up to be a man.

Vacations are definitely educational. You learn a lot spending two weeks in a compact car with the ones you thought you loved most.

No legacy is so rich as honesty.

Children are the only people wise enough to enjoy today without regretting yesterday or fearing tomorrow.

Statistics clearly point out that most family problems are relatives.

Every husband and wife knows that when one loses his temper the other catches it.

Set your hopes for the young no higher than your example.

Children have never been very good at listening to their elders, but they have never failed to imitate them.

All journeys fall into one of two categories, to home or from home.

When mom is mad at dad, don't let her brush your hair.

The finest home entertainment center is a happy child of three.

An optimist is a father who is willing to let a teenage son take the new car on a date; a pessimist is one who isn't, and a cynic is one who did.

Despite the number of people in a family, a mother's opinion constitutes a majority.

Parents never fully appreciate teachers until it rains all weekend.

Videos have not only replaced radio for teenagers - they've done a pretty good job on homework, too.

The girl who married a man to mend his ways is likely to learn he isn't worth a darn.

A marriage license, like a fishing license, doesn't guarantee a prize catch.

A truly happy marriage is one in which the woman gives the best years of her life to the man who makes them the best years.

Any child raised strictly by the book is probably a first edition.

Things balance out - your friends troubles aren't as bad as yours, but your relatives are worse.

Making a marriage work is a lot like farming; it requires constant attention, seven days and nights each week.

Is it not strange that he who has no children brings them up so well? The ability to speak distinguishes us from the lower animals. What we say frequently doesn't.

Many parents don't dare help their children with homework for fear the kids will find out how little they know

So what if the grass is so much greener on the other side of the fence? Chances are, you wouldn't want their water bill.

The only time a husband can be sure he's right is when he admits he's wrong.

Anybody who has been married more than 10 minutes has had to forgive somebody for something.

What parents leave in their children is more important than what they leave to them.

Everybody makes mistakes, but husbands learn about them sooner.

A fifth-grade boy wrote in an essay: "I have enjoyed my boyhood so much that I am looking forward to my adultery."

The one thing marriage manuals should state as gospel fact, squeezing toothpaste in the middle is considered a hostile act.

Economists report that a college education adds many thousands of dollars to a man's lifetime income - which he then spends sending his children to college.

Remember that children, marriages, and flower gardens reflect the kind of care they get.

Small drops, tiny spills, scattered crumbs across the floor. The dog's job: clean up!

As long as your wife tries to improve your table manners, your grammar, your posture, your attire and station in life, you know at least, that she still loves you.

Few men believe in dreams after they marry one.

In these times, the accent is on youth - but the stress usually is on the parents.

A treasure - A truly priceless work of art is a child loved from the heart.

A woman smart enough to ask a man's advice is usually not dumb enough to take it.

"Never forget your wife's birthday - and never remember which one it is."

Parents should learn to laugh at themselves after all, their kids do.

We have to live beyond our means; our kids were born with designers genes.

Psychiatrists tell us women tend to marry men like their fathers. Now we know why mothers cry at weddings.

In-laws play an important role in any family. They're so useful for demonstrating who one's naughty children take after.

All work and no play is dad's version of his childhood.

I wish my wife would finish her holiday shopping. I'm dying to know what I got her.

Due to the high price of games. Toys-r-Us is expanding its service to include an adult lounge called Woe-is-Me.

So you're lost little man," said the lady, 'Why didn't you hang onto your mother's skirt?"
Said the youngster, "Couldn't reach it."

An advantage of poverty: Your relatives gain nothing by your death.

Sometimes the worst children are the so-called adults.

Christmas is when family ties bring people together, and they come in all sizes and colors.

The teenager who gets a few dollars from dad expects mom to provide matching funds.

Family reunions are when people travel from the four corners of the earth to get together with all the relatives they've moved to the four corners of the earth to get away from.

The marriage counselor said he wanted to hear both sides of the story, so she told him.

Mother to young daughter, "Of course your father remembers his senior prom, that's why he wants you home by eleven."

The quickest way to learn how to do it yourself is to criticize your wife doing it.

I got my wife a microwave. Now she ruins my meals in half the time.

Be it ever so costly, there's no place like home.

Marry you and take your name? Are you crazy? I don't want people to call me Fred!

During 2am feedings, many new parents find themselves wondering where the saying 'Sleep like a baby' came from.

Where there's a well, there's a flock of hungry relatives.

My mother-in-law comes every Christmas and stays until the New Year. Don't complain. My Mother-in-law comes every New Year and stays until Christmas.

Nothing can make the family car look depreciated more than having a neighbor who buys a new one.

A grandparent is someone who gives you money, but doesn't make you clean your room.

Gifts from relatives and friends are usually of two types: those you don't like and those you don't get.

The boyfriend looked into his girlfriend's eyes and said: "I can look into a girl's eyes and tell exactly what she thinks of me." "Well that must be very discouraging", she replied.

My husband graciously opened the car door for me, unfortunately, we were going 60 M.P.H. at the time.

When two people marry they become as one. The trouble begins when they try to decide which one.

The family you come from isn't as important as the family you're going to have.

Who says today's children don't know the meaning of punishment? Some of them are sure good enough at dishing it out to their parents.

It is not always wise to shake a family tree. You don't know what kind of nuts will fall out.

A brat is a child who acts like your own, but belongs to a neighbor.

It should give parents great comfort in knowing that someday their teenagers will grow to know as little as they do.

The quickest way to find out what's on your wife's mind is to sit yourself down in a comfortable chair.

Stress is hereditary. Parents can get it from their children.

A chaperon is an elderly woman who accompanies young women to see that they do not indulge in any of the things she would have indulged in if she hadn't been chaperoned when she was young.

Happy is the man who marries a good cook, has good digestion, and a fat bank account.

A little boy called to the new neighbor and said, "If you are annoyed by the piano playing next door, be sure and complain to my mother."

Behind every successful man you'll find a woman who has nothing to wear.

Children are natural mimics. They act like their parents despite every attempt by grown-ups to teach them good manners.

The best way to praise your mate is often.

It is better to have loved and lost - provided no alimony is involved.

A wife lasts only for the length of the marriage, but an ex-wife is there for the rest of your life.

Home is where others rarely say they love you, but deep down in your heart you know they do.

Many parents work hard and save their money so their children won't have the same problems that made mature adults of their parents.

Nothing strikes terror in the heart of the experienced husband like the words, "We have to talk."

After the kids leave home, some parents suffer from the empty nest syndrome; others change the locks.

You can say this for these ready mixes, the next generation isn't going to have any trouble making cakes exactly like mother used to make.

Raising children is like playing golf. You keep thinking you'll do better the next time.

If family members really expressed how they felt, more in-laws would be outlaws.

Before most people start boasting about their family tree, they usually do a good pruning job.

"They say two out of three mattresses bought in America last longer than the marriages?

"I thing it's important for one to start off with a good first marriage."

Our divorce rate might be lower if we spent as much time preparing for the marriage as we do for the wedding.

The quickest way to learn how to do it yourself is to criticize the way your wife is doing it.

Children are small creatures who make parents old and grandparents young.

Men usually love women for what they are.
Women usually love men for what they might be.

Why be down on your parents? They did not have a choice either.

These days lots of teenagers are getting married, expecting their folks to be good supports about it.

Why should you never marry a tennis player? Love means nothing to them.

Some people ask the secret of our long marriage. We take time to go to a restaurant two times a week. A little candlelight, dinner, soft music and dancing. She goes Tuesdays, I go Fridays.

About the only two things a young child will share willingly are contagious diseases and parental secrets.

When you have a teenage son who wears makeup and purple hair, federal deficits are a minor problem.

A child can take 'no' for an answer, but not very seriously.

Marriage is a high stakes game. If you lose, you have to come up with alimony. If you win, you have to come up with violin lessons, orthodontist payments, and college tuition.

A happy home is where both mates think they got better than they deserve.

Nobody will ever win the battle of the sexes. There's too much fraternizing with the enemy.

Men and women may never learn much about the opposite sex, but we have a lot of fun trying.

He that speaks ill of his wife dishonors himself.

A man can let his wife know he loves her with a dozen long stemmed roses; his small son can do the same with a fistful of dandelions.

It's terrifying to speculate in what the children of the next generation will have to do to shock their parents.

The easiest thing to overlook in a family is how much we need each other.

All parents should save something for a rainy day, like patience.

Juvenile delinquency begins when children stop asking their mom and dad where they came from and start telling them where to go.

In a courtship the heart beats so loudly: it blocks out the sound from the mind.

Today's teenagers know the value of a dollar; that's why they have so little respect for it.

Teenagers suffer from knowing pains.

Old school thinking: There are some children who should be applauded with just one hand.

Some relatives are like fires; the sooner they're out, the better.

Most American children get the best of everything, including their parents.

An altar is a place where a bachelor loses control of himself.

Ask a kid what the grand in grandparents describes, and the immediate answer will be. "The presents they give."

When a man makes a woman his wife, it's the highest compliment he can pay for her and it's usually the last.

It's claimed that redheads have more violent tempers than blondes or brunettes, but my wife has been all three and I can't tell the difference.

Who was braver than Lancelot, wiser than Socrates, more honorable than Lincoln, wittier than Mark Twain, and more handsome than Apollo?
My wife's first husband.

The trouble with relaxing in your own home is that no matter where you sit it seems you're looking at something that you should be doing.

The best way to wake up with a smile on your face is to go to bed with one already there.

The family is the test of freedom; because the family is the only thing that the free man makes for himself and by himself.

Children keep on the straight and narrow best if they get good road directions from people who have traveled the route.

Getting married is a good deal like going into a restaurant with friends. You order what you want, then when you see what the other fellow has and you wish you had taken that.

Years ago people got married, but they couldn't stand living together. Today people live together, but they can't stand getting married.

Family reunions leave us with precious memories, and fuel for thought.

There are two kinds of wives, those who look forward to their husbands coming home from work and others who look forward to them going to work.

It isn't grooming as much as character that makes a woman a lady.

Good parents teach their children, wise ones learn from them.

Be kind to your mother-in-law, babysitters are expensive.

A full cabin is better than an empty castle.

A mother's patience is like a tube of toothpaste - it's never quite all gone.

Marriage changes passion, suddenly you're in bed with a relative.

Let there be space in your togetherness.

By the time many a man realizes that maybe his father was right, he has a son who thinks he is wrong.

Ask your child what he wants for dinner only if he's buying.

The more I go though parenting, the more I say I owe my mother an apology.

I asked my husband if he wanted to renew our vows, he got so excited, he thought they had expired.

Children are like wet cement, whatever falls on them make an impression.

Be nice to your kids, they pick your nursing home.

We must teach our children to dream with their eyes.

They say marriages are made in heaven, but so are thunder and lightning.

A mother never realizes that her children are no longer children.

There are only two things a child will share willingly, communicable diseases and his mother's age.

Wrinkles are hereditary. Parents get them from their children.

The only time a woman really listens to her husband is when he talks in his sleep.

A genius is often a stupid kid with very happy grandparents.

The neighbors have a car that is so old it has been paid for.

Too many people serve turkey, yams, dressing, and pickled relatives during the Holidays.

Nothing makes a boy smarter than being a grandson.

Treat your spouse's family as you would like them to treat yours.

Home is where your spouse and children live. Until then, a house is only a building.

In marriage, being the right person is just as important as finding the right person.

Where there's a will, there's a relative.

Your kitchen isn't clean until your sink is clean.

Most people won't see the rest of your house, but they'll surely take home an impression of you from your front door.

Keep your house clean enough to keep the health department away, and cluttered enough so it looks lived in.

If your bed is made and your dishes washed, your house is in good shape.

An ugly darn is better than a pretty hole.

Ask yourself, "Would I say or do this if mom were looking over my shoulder?"

Remember who you are and where you come from.

Boys on the mind is worse than water on the brain.

Said about any young girl who won't settle down with a nice man - "She's going to fly all around the pretty birds and land in a cow pile".

Do as I say, not as I do.

If you don't behave, I'm going to jump down your throat and kick".

I want you to straighten up and act like you have a little sense, whether you do or not.

I'll always love you, but sometimes I don't like you.

You made your bed, so go lie in it.

If you wish to be treated as a lady, you must act like a lady. Be a lady, no matter how painful.

It doesn't matter what's on the outside, as long as you have a lady's heart.

Best to wear clothes tight enough to show you're a girl, but loose enough to show you're a lady.

Always remember, it isn't the way the outside of a house looks, but what goes on inside.

When a child is born, so is a grandmother.

Having a young child explain something exciting he has seen is the finest example of communication you will ever see or hear.

Marriage is like anything else in life that is challenging... The harder you work, the luckier you get.

Having a mate who nags is good for your health.

One day I decided not to let unimportant things annoy me, so I asked her to move out.

Sometimes it takes 20 years for a child to hear what a parent tells him.

Train a child in the way he should grow, and walk there yourself once in a while.

Grandkids are God's reward for our having survived parenthood.

A retired husband is a wife's full-time job.

Thrift is a wonderful virtue - especially in an ancestor.

Autumn colors make mom mellow, and none so much as school-bus yellow.

Few things are more satisfying than seeing your children have teenagers of their own.

Some people can trace their ancestry back hundreds of years, but cannot tell you where their children were last night.

The shortest distance between two points is through the neighbor's backyard.

Wife to husband - I miss that morning newspaper you used to hold in front of your face.

Why does the cooing stop after the honeymoon, but the billing goes on forever?

Marriage and Family

Things don't come to you until you're ready - except children.

My father can beat up your father!
Big deal. So can my mother!

If you think the grass is greener in your neighbor's yard, then let him worry about cutting it.

It may be clothes that make the man, but it's usually the woman who picks them out.

What do you mean I never say anything good about your mother? Didn't I just say 'good riddance'?

Wife who nags too much - may have a husband who horses around.

Teenagers have a lot of hang-ups, but you'd never know it by looking4n. their closets.

I wasn't always depressed. I had everything, power, wealth, the love of a beautiful woman, and then my wife found out.

There are two periods in life when a man thinks seriously about marriage before the wedding and before the divorce.

Plumber to housewife: "I've found your problem - it's your husband."

The next time you're tempted to criticize your wife's judgment, just remember she married you,

Man: "I'd like some flowers for my wife.
What can I get for five dollars?'
Florist: "How about some seeds?"

I learned in school today that my teacher can read lips.

The neighbor's grass may be greener, but their water bills are higher too.

The only thing that makes a woman happy about putting on an old dress is the fact that she still can.

Two's company; three's the result.

The difference between parents and grandparents is that parents usually "NO" better.

Marriage is an expensive way to get free advice.

Most of the things I liked to do as a kid now are being done by batteries.

I'm enjoying my grandchildren so much I wish I'd had them first.

Woman can keep a secret just as well as men, it just takes more of them to do it.

Christmas toys are most educational. They teach kids that adults will buy almost anything.

School days are the happiest days of your life, provided of course, your kids are old enough to go.

Sooner or later every bad little kid gets what's coming to him; he grows up and becomes a parent.

Bachelors have no idea what married bliss is, and that's also true of a lot of husbands.

Any fair-minded man has to be for equality of the sexes, but it'll be a cold day in hell before women let us have it.

Some of us can remember when all kitchen tools were cordless.

A woman is the only hunter who uses herself for bait.

Today's teenagers believe they have a right to life, liberty and a car suitable for the pursuit of happiness.

I never ran away from home as a kid, of course, I never did anything else my parents wanted me to do, either.

Home is that warm feeling you get when you walk in the door and everyone ignores you.

Chivalry is man's instinct to protect women from everyone but himself.

Two women met - one said to the other, "Do you have any children?"
"No"
"So what do you do for aggravation?"

Most marriages are not made in heaven; they come in HIS and HER kits and have to be put together.

"I switched on the late show last night and the movie was so old the girl said 'no'.

Marriage is the only thing that affords a woman the pleasure of company and the perfect sensation of solitude at the same time.

The reason there are so many June weddings is that it's hard to think in the heat.

Marriage will always be popular. There is no other state in which an adult can be certain that someone is worrying about him and wishing him well while being mad at him at the same time.

Getting kids up for school in the morning is the day's biggest challenge.

Marriage is proof that people can take a joke.

Family harmony takes understanding, patience and at least two TV sets.

Thank heaven genes were discovered; now we have an excuse for almost everything.

Marriage is like a lottery. The only trouble is, you can't tear up your ticket if you lose.

Some bachelors balk at getting married because they think the word 'husband' sounds to close to 'has been'.

Have you heard about that new kind of home entertainment? It's called conversation.

All forms of gambling are frowned upon by preachers, except marriage.

Marriage is for those who don't like eating leftovers alone.

Nothing makes a woman look better than three cocktails inside a man.

Feminists know what kind of man they want to marry. The problem is there aren't enough wimps to go around.

Stand up to your spouse, or all is lost; he who hesitates is bossed!

The lady who remembers her first kiss has a grand-daughter who can't remember her first husband.

The urge to run away from home usually strikes us twice: when you are 15 and when your child is.

A commitment to marriage these days is 'until disappointments'.

Christmas is a wonderful day for children. For parents, peace on earth comes a few days later when all the batteries wear out.

Ever notice how nothing changes the color of paint like putting it on a wall.

Marriage is dedicated to the proposition that all men are berated equal.

A conversation between two children. "I found a contraceptive on the patio last night."
"What's a patio?" said the other.

A woman never knows what kind of husband she doesn't want until she marries him.

Isn't it strange that God's masterpiece, an infant, can be produced by unskilled labor?

After a man gets married it doesn't take him long to learn that half of the time she's right and the other half he's wrong.

Paying alimony is like having the TV set on after you have fallen asleep.

Men love mystery stories, That's why women fascinate them.

Wife to husband: Go easy on the drinks, telling dirty stories, and flirting with the girls. Just have a good time.

For parents, a good rule of thumb is - don't try to keep your kids under it.

I have a glowworm marriage - the glow is gone, but the worm remains.

Most unruly children have a lot to be spankful for.

One big difference between outlaws and in-laws is that outlaws don't promise to pay it back.

A husband who gets breakfast in bed is usually in the hospital.

Marriages are not made in heaven. They are do-it-yourself kits with no instructions.

Teenager's idea of a clean room is one where you can find the phone by the second ring.

A well-knit family is one where everybody gives a darn.

When we break a promise to a child, we are starting to break the bond of confidence that the child has with us.

If it weren't for teenagers, some of us would never realize our shortcomings as parents.

Grandparents and grandchildren understand each other because they know how to outwit the generation between them.

A family vacation is when you take along everyone you need the vacation from.

Any household task is fascinating to a child until he's old enough to do it.

You never fully appreciate the value of education until vacation is over and the kids are back in school.

Man, pressing MUTE button on remote control; "I wish this worked on my wife instead of the TV."

It's easy enough to be happy when there isn't a jolt or a jar,
But the father worthwhile is a man who can sidle
When his teenager's driving his car.

The joy of motherhood is what a woman experiences when the kids are in bed.

Bad music is the kind our kids like. Good music is the kind we liked when we were kids.

An old-fashioned woman is a gal who tries to make one husband last a lifetime.

Orr's Laws

Orr's Laws

I take candy from strangers.

Enjoy the little things. One day you may look back and realize that they were the big things.

When someone tells you, he will think it over and let you know"
You know.

Some people always seem to have enough gas for an ego trip.

Look for the humor in the serious, the joy in the sad, the strength in the weak and the best in the bad.

The only way to win, an argument is not to begin it.

"Girls have unfair advantage over men. If they can't get what they want by being smart, they can get it by being dumb."

Anyone who is in condition to jog doesn't have to.

Nothing makes you feel older than finding the racy novel you once hid in the closet on your kid's required reading list.

For every problem there is a solution - even if it's learning to live with the problem.

Love not returned is like a garden without sunshine.

Most of what you hear on the grapevine comes from sour grapes.

The lottery was invented to give the unlucky a chance to support the lucky.

Just because the river is quiet, don't think the crocodiles have left.

You're still young at middle age, but only once in a while.

Talent is a flame. Genius is a fire.

Doing your best is more important than being the best.

Anyone who is pulling his weight has none left over to throw around.

Let us choose to believe something good can happen.

It is more important to do the right thing than to do things right.

A conscience is the price of morality, and morality is the price of civilization.

Doubt anything but yourself.

Patience unlocks the door to achievement.

Things accomplish nothing - people accomplish everything.

The difference between winning and losing is self-discipline.

It isn't how much you spend, it's what you do with it.

Victory belongs to the most persevering.

If you are going to get in over your head, it might be a good idea to first learn how to swim.

Nothing is achieved before it is thoroughly attempted.

Destiny is not a matter of chance; it is a matter of choice.

To try is commendable. To try when you know you will probably fail is magnificent.

To hurt someone you know will forgive you is the unkindest thing of all.

It's what we learn after we know it all that really counts.

One of the most expensive things around is a free catalog.

If you can't tell the difference, what difference does it make.

Mistakes are a lot like credit cards, sooner or later you have to pay for them.

You won't understand God's love until you've felt compassion for somebody you didn't like.

Carrying a grudge requires energy that could be used to help carry another's load.

History celebrates few persons who waited for inspiration.

Orr's Laws

We never really appreciate the sun, friends or liberty until they are gone.

The older you get, the older you want to get.

When something is said to be easier said than done, it's seldom done?

Bragging doesn't help get the job done anymore than the whistle helps the train get up hill.

Don't ever admit your faults. You leave no pleasure for your friends who love pointing them out.

It's better to be a has-been than a never-was.

Exercising charity strengthens the muscles of the soul.

Act quickly, think slowly.

Although crime doesn't pay, it does provide free room and board if you're caught.

Cosmetics may improve on Mother Nature, but they can never fool Father Time

Remember that all news is biased.

If you are pure of heart and eat your Wheaties, good things can happen to you.

Don't expect different results from the same behavior.

Listen to your critics. They will keep you focused and innovative.

Remember the deal's not done until the check has cleared the bank.

In matters of principle, listen to your conscience and not the crowd.

The best way to go up in the world is to be up before the rest of the world starts going.

Anyone who has time to look for a four leaf clover deserves to find one.

If you keep trying, destiny may get tired of watching you and give you a victory.

You are never taller than when you stoop to help another human being to his feet.

A job worth doing is worth doing well, and if you do it well, you'll probably be stuck with it forever.

Give a man a fish, and he eats for a day. Teach him to fish, and you get rid of him for the weekend.

It is not against the law to be stupid, but it's stupid to be against the law.

Rule of thumb: If you're the one with the hammer, get somebody else to hold the nail.

When there's a will, there's a way. Where there's a won't there isn't.

A person should judge his success by whether it also helped others succeed.

Make someone happy today, mind your own business.

Dresses should be tight enough to show you are a woman and loose enough to show you're a lady.

Any fool can point but your faults, and most of them will.

A good scare is worth more to man than good advice.

Self-confidence comes from others having confidence in us.

Don't fret if you can't see the light at the end of the tunnel. Be glad you can see the tunnel.

If you can't apologize, you'd better be good at making new friends.

The surest way to have the last word is to apologize.

As soon as you're satisfied with your ability it has begun to decline.

The true measure of an individual is how he treats a person who can do him absolutely no good.

Whether you think health or wealth is more important depends upon which one you've lost.

Courage isn't having the strength to go on; it's going on when you don't have the strength.

The greatest sermons are lived—not preached.

We all leave footprints in the sands of time - either a great soul or a heel.

There is no man who is not capable of doing more than he thinks he can do.

A truthful recognition of our own ignorance is a foot on the doorstep to the temple of wisdom.

The right to be heard is constitutional. The right to be listened to must be earned.

A compliment is verbal sunshine.

Indifference often is a more obnoxious response than criticism.

We reach for perfection, but we should pray that we do not get it. For if we do, to what can we then reach?

Don't talk about things you know nothing about. People may think you're running for office.

The greatest test of strength is whether you can shoulder another's burden.

A thousand words will not leave so deep an impression as one deed.

Those who don't try anything new are apt to grow old quickly.

The amount of sleep required by the average person is usually five minutes more.

It is not wrong to have success, money, and the material comforts of life. What is wrong is to have them and not care that others do not.

Confidence, like the soul never returns once it has departed.

Blowing one's own horn only tends to deafen the listener.

It is more important to think what you say than say what you think.

The key to willpower is want power. People who want something badly enough can usually find the willpower to achieve it.

A sorrow shared is a sorrow halved.

The kindest word in the world is the unkind word unsaid.

You needn't tell people what you know, they can tell by the things you do.

Thought is a guide to action, not a substitute for it.

One way to encourage others is simply to stop finding fault.

One hand helping is worth two applauding.

You cannot solve a problem if you're thinking on the same level you were when you created the problem.

The greatest test of courage is to bear defeat without losing heart.

If you judge people, you have no time to love them.

The most exquisite pleasure is giving pleasure to others.

The best remedy for a short temper is a long walk.

When it comes to-flattery, nothing succeeds like excess.

Look out for the fellow who lets you do all the talking.

Experience is not what happens to you; it is what you do with what happens to you.

Anxiety is interest paid on trouble before it falls due.

Hating people is like burning down your own house to get rid of a rat.

Nothing is ever a total failure - it can always serve as a bad example.

Beware of Prejudices. They are like rats, and men's minds are like traps; prejudices get in easily, but it is doubtful if they ever get out.

Just because you find fault doesn't mean you have to report it.

He that respects himself is safe from others; He wears a coat of mail that none can pierce.

Morality is like paint, it is no good until it is applied.

If there be any truer measure of a man than by what he does, it must be by what he gives.

Where you go hereafter depends largely on what you go after here.

If you want to know what people really think of you, make them angry.

People who never play golf will lie about other things.

A hundred loads of worry will not pan an ounce of debt.

If at first you don't succeed, hire yourself out as a consultant.

If you do what you've always done, you'll get what you've always got.

The truth shall make you free, but first it shall make you pretty uncomfortable.

Most effective smoke detector around is the nose of somebody who's trying to quit.

Conversation is the art of telling people a little less than they want to know.

You are making progress if each mistake you make is a new one.

In dealing with people, always be prepared to go the extra smile.

Don't be afraid to be vulnerable. If you don't open the door, how can anyone come in?

Slow to anger and quick to forgive and you will have friends as long as you live.

If you want your dreams to come true, you have to stay wide awake.

Courtesy is contagious. This country could do with an epidemic.

The rung of a ladder was never meant to rest upon, but only hold a man's foot long enough to enable him to put the other somewhat higher.

Luck, bad if not good, will always be with us, but it has a way of favoring the intelligent and showing its back to the stupid.

Cooked-up excuses usually sound half-baked.

It is better to keep your mouth shut. If you talk about yourself you're a bore; if you talk about others, you're a gossip.

You can easily judge the character of a man by how he treats those who can do nothing for him or to him.

Some people are molded by their admirations, others by their hostilities.

Be not disturbed at being misunderstood; be disturbed rather at not being understanding.

Don't do the crime if you can't do the time.

Envy eats nothing but it's own heart.

If you hear that a mountain has moved, believe, but if you hear that a man has changed his character, believe it not.

What is so important and so often overlooked in any difference of opinion is that it's not what is wrong, but what is right.

Reason is rarely eloquent enough to control emotion.

Emotion is a sprint man, but character is a marathon runner.

It only takes the breath of gossip to snuff out the candle of truth.

It is the fresh egg that gets slapped in the pan.

We can choose to growl, scowl, and criticize, or enjoy, employ, and harmonize.

Think before you speak.

Yelling at people to get them to do things your way makes about as much sense as driving your car by honking your horn.

There's no one so wise as the person who says nothing at the right time.

The things most people want to know about are usually none of their business.

A grouch is a guy who has himself signed up and is sore about it.

A man can fall many times, but he isn't a failure until he begins to blame somebody else.

Anyone who's all wrapped up in himself is overdressed.

Many troubles of the world would be solved if we all worked as hard as we think everyone else should.

To live is to change, and to be perfect is to have changed often.

On the win/loss record of your life, try to do better than break even.

Orr's Laws

Do something bad and regret it. Do something good and forget it.

Live in such a way that you would not be ashamed to sell your parrot to the town gossip.

The journey is the reward.

The key to everything is patience. You get the chicken by hatching the egg, not by smashing it.

Man is most nearly himself when he achieves the seriousness of a child at play.

Don't rock the boat.

He who conquers others is strong; he who conquers himself is mighty.

If you want to find perfection, don't look in the mirror.

Passion is energy. Feed the power that comes from focusing on what excites you.

For fast-acting relief, try slowing down.

It isn't necessary to blow out the other person's light to let your own shine.

Be all you can be.

The person who takes responsibility on his shoulders isn't likely to have a chip there.

Luck is where preparation meets with opportunity.

People who sing their own praises are apt to be soloists.

Always keep you head up, but be careful to keep your nose on a friendly level.

Silence is never insincere.

Reaching high keeps people on their toes.

If you want a place in the sun, you must leave the shade of the family tree.

It often takes more courage to change one's opinion than to stick to it.

When you are angry, sing.

Don't meet trouble halfway, it is quite capable of making the entire journey.

Write injuries in sand, kindness in marble.

Change your thoughts, and you change your world.

The easiest way to get to sleep is to count your blessings instead of your problems.

Get knocked down seven times. Get up eight times.

No one can make you feel inferior without your consent.

If you are too big to do small jobs; you are too small to do big jobs.

Always wear a smile.

Do your best, Angels can do no better.

If you want to leave your footprints in the sands of time, wear work shoes.

Don't ever slam a door - you might want to go back.

Ignore those who try to discourage you.

Wearing perfume doesn't take the place of a bath or shower.

Wash down as far as possible; then up as far as possible; then wash possible.

Soap is cheap and water is plentiful, so there's no excuse for going dirty.

Don't rattle like an empty wagon.

If you cannot do great things, do small things in a great way.

Change your thoughts, and you change your world.

If your plans get changed, make some new ones.

Bloom where you are planted.

Do it and be glad that you are able.

Don't speak in haste when you're upset, or you'll say things that you'll regret.

Don't do anything that wouldn't make happy memories.

Use it up, wear it out, make it do, or go without.

In action, be primitive; in foresight, a strategist.

The test of any man lies in action.

Discretion is the better part of valor.

Don't wait for your ship to come in - swim out to it.

Don't blow with the wind.

Let your conscience be your guide.

Before you decide to accept a new idea as your own, try it on to see if it fits.

Pick your apples from the top of the tree; any old apple will fall.

Don't jump out of the frying pan into the fire.

Take one step at a time.

If you always tell the truth you will never have to remember what you said.

Do all the good you can, by all the means you can, in all the ways you can, in all the places you can, at all the times you can, to all the people you can, as long as ever you can.

Knowledge and Wisdom

Knowledge and Wisdom

If you learn something new every day—the days are not wasted.

Two ears and one mouth may mean that you should listen twice as much as you talk.

Intelligence without ambition is a bird without wings.

Emotion has taught people to reason.

If you don't use your head a little, you'll have to use your heels a lot.

Teach someone to read. Change a life.

Anyone who stops learning is old, whether this happens at age 80 or 20.

If you have knowledge let others light their candles in it.

A man only learns in two ways; one by reading and the other by association with smarter people.

There is no knowledge that is not power.

Young folks ought to know that old folks know more about being young than they know about being old.

An unusual amount of common sense is sometimes called wisdom.

Wonder rather than doubt, is the root of knowledge.

Whenever one acquires knowledge but does not practice it, it is like one who ploughs a field but does not sow it.

Wonder, rather than doubt, is the root of knowledge.

A bookstore is one of the only pieces of evidence we have that people are still thinking.

The ability to speak more than one language is an asset, but the knack of keeping a mouth shut in any language is equally valuable.

Believing you can get smarter can actually make you more knowledgeable.

You don't know what you know until you find out what you don't know.

An open mind collects more riches than an open purse.

Creativity is allowing yourself to make mistakes. Art is knowing which ones to keep.

Wisdom is a treasure no robber can touch.

A mind once expanded by a new idea, never returns to its original dimensions.

Minds are like parachutes - they only function when open.

Good teachers are the ones who are able to challenge young minds without losing their own.

Rumors are so spreadable, it's incredible.

The cure for boredom is curiosity, for which there is no cure.

One can no more gain proficiency by resting on a job than he can acquire knowledge by sitting on a dictionary.

Knowing others is wisdom; knowing yourself is enlightenment.

The world does not pay for what a person knows, but it pays for what a person does with what he knows.

No wise man ever wished to be younger.

Intellectuals solve problems; geniuses prevent them.

It isn't how much you know, but what you get done that the world remembers.

Learn from your mistakes and your education will be boundless.

Like a rubber band, the truth weakens the more it is stretched.

If you want truly to understand something. Try to change it.

Education is the best provision for old age.

The best service a book can render you is; not to impart truth; but to make you think it out for yourself.

The recipe for perpetual ignorance is: Be satisfied with your opinions and content with your knowledge.

Doubt is the key to knowledge.

Nobody who can read is ever successful at cleaning out an attic.

Honesty is the first chapter in the book of wisdom.

Reading is to the mind what exercise is to the body.

To act as we should is the moral part; to know how to act is the intellectual part.

Fools need advice most, but wise men only are the better for it.

The only way to keep your education is to give it away.

Intelligence is recognizing a flaw in your boss' reasoning. Wisdom is refraining from pointing it out.

The advantage of college lies in stimulus, and not in information. The stimulus we need, but the information we can get through a clerk.

The cost of education is high - about one tenth of the cost of ignorance.

Imagination is more important than knowledge

How many grad students does it take to change a light bulb?
Only one - but it takes years and years.

They give you a B.A. when you think you know everything, an M.A. when you realize you know nothing, and a Ph.D. when you learn that nobody else knows anything either.

Intelligence will never win a race unless it is driven by enthusiasm.

I learn more by listening, after all, anything I would say I already know.

Trying to get an education from the classroom alone is like eating a cookbook.

Employ your time in improving yourself by other men's writings so that you shall come easily by what others have labored hard for.

He who does not read is condemned to see the world through only one pair of eyes.

Education is like a zero. By itself, it means nothing, but it can add a lot to what's already there.

What wisdom can you find that is greater than kindness?

A brilliant person is one who knows when to say nothing.

A man of knowledge lives by acting, not thinking about acting.

All wise people share one trait - the ability to listen.

The courage to speak must be matched by the wisdom to listen.

The person who knows everything has a lot to learn.

Good listeners are not only popular but, after awhile, they know a few things.

A prudent question is one half of wisdom.

If your mind should go blank - don't forget to turn off the sound.

Nurture your mind with great thoughts; to believe in the heroic makes heroes.

No matter how long he lives, no man ever becomes as wise as the average woman of forty-eight.

The true test of a first rate mind is the ability to hold two contradictory ideas at the same time.

The creative mind is the playful mind.

Philosophy is the play and dance of ideas.

Love of beauty is taste. The creation of beauty is art.

Experience is the best teacher.

God gave us two ears and one mouth. He wanted us to listen more than we talk.

A still tongue makes a wise head.

Get all the education you can in your lifetime, because no one can ever take that away from you.

Knowledge and Wisdom

A book is like a garden carried in the pocket.

I hear and I forget. I see and I remember. I do and I understand.

Knowledge and timber should not be much used till they are seasoned.

Give yourself a time of quiet to learn some good thing.

Praise without noise; be learned without display.

Never rest until you get at the reasons for what you notice is going on around you; investigate, learn.

Never try to tell everything you know. It may take too short a time.

Let us never, never doubt what nobody is sure about.

A dram of discretion is worth a pound of wisdom.

All the mind's activity is easy if it is not subjected to reality.

Good intentions are useless in the absence of common sense.

The finding of arguments for a conclusion given in advance is not philosophy, but special pleading.

Wise people will use the ideas of others as well as and in addition to their own.

The best way to improve your memory is to lend someone else money.

There can be no wisdom disjoined from goodness.

It takes lots of things to show you're smart, but only one thing to prove you're not.

"That bottle of magic potion you sold me was supposed to make me smarter. I'm beginning to think I was swindled."
"See there? You're smarter already".

A lot of mistakes would not have happened if folks had known as much as they thought they did.

I learn more by listening, after all, anything I would say I already know.

A little experience can help a person overcome quite a bit of education.

An expert is like the bottom half of a double boiler. It lets off a lot of steam, but it really doesn't know what's cooking.

Receiving too much advice makes the decision more difficult.

The man who knows everybody's business is usually neglecting his own.

Don't listen to someone because he has a degree unless it's a degree of common sense.

TV game shows can be educational. Every time someone turns one on, go into another room and read.

It is not how much book learning you've stuffed in your head that counts. What does count is how you use all the stuff you've stuffed.

I'm always fascinated by the way memory diffuses fact.

The only good is knowledge and the only evil ignorance.

Real wisdom is the ability to avoid any situation that requires it.

A person's education continues only as long as his ignorance is exceeded by his curiosity.

Hearing is a gift; listening is an art.

Ignorance is a prison, and some people never come up for parole.

Every time you open your mouth, you expose your brains.

Ph.D., 'Piled high and deep'.

The margin of error we allow for other's mistakes is as narrow or wide as our own mind.

Many receive advice, only the wise profit from it.

A young man knows the rules, but an old man knows the exceptions.

Dwell on defeats only long enough to learn from them.

The easiest person to fool is the fellow who knows it all.

If you understand the problem, it isn't a problem.

A great many people mistake opinions for thoughts.

Knowledge and Wisdom

A million facts do not necessarily add up to wisdom.

An intellectual is someone who can listen to the William Tell Overture and not think of the Lone Ranger.

A genius does not think of his field of expertise as work.

Education's purpose is to replace an empty mind with an open one.

A great teacher never strives to explain his vision - he simply invites you to stand beside him and see for yourself.

Vision is the art of seeing things invisible.

A man of knowledge lives by acting, not by thinking about acting.

Be curious always, for knowledge will not acquire you; you must acquire it.

Trust your hunches. They're usually based on facts filed away just below the conscious level.

Statistics are no substitute for judgment.

Education is learning what you didn't even know you didn't know.

A mind once stretched by a new idea, never regains its original dimensions.

Politics

187

Politics

Liberty is an impartial lady. If we convince her to abolish freedom for others she may do it for us.

Teacher: "Helen, what are the three great American parties? Helen: "Democratic, Republican and Tupperware."

One of the things we have to be thankful for is that we don't get as much government as we pay for.

They can conquer who believe they can.

It isn't necessary for a politician to fool all the people all the time. A majority on Election Day is enough.

I am from the government; I'm here to help you?

Election time is when the new candidates come around to tell us how stupid we were to vote for the winners last time.

The first thing a politician learns is to keep a swivel tongue in his head.

The tough economic situation is affecting everybody. Last week organized crime had to lay off ten judges.

Why does a slight tax increase cost you $200 and a substantial tax cut saves you thirty cents?

The more we listen to political speeches, the more we realize why this country is called "the land of promise".

Bureaucracy is when the first person who answers the phone can't help you.

The welfare of the people is the highest law.

Plans are underway - in twenty years, they're going to have a Soviet Re-Union.

Incumbents are just politicians who make the same mistakes twice.

A taxpayer is someone who doesn't have to pass a civil service exam to work for the government.

The trouble with our economy is this - While we are earning money five days a week, the government is spending it seven.

If at first you don't succeed, take the tax loss.

Have you noticed as the world gets smaller how it takes more tax to keep it together?

IRS Commissioner to head Red Cross - says getting blood from people should be no problem.

It's no exaggeration to say the undecided could go one way or another.

Voters were divided into two groups this year: those who wanted to bring back the capital gains tax, end those who wanted to bring back capital gains.

Chicago voters were so upset, they only voted once.

Mothers all want their sons to grow up to be President, but they don't want them to become politicians in the process.

Politics is the ability to foretell what is going to happen tomorrow, next week, next month and next year and to have the ability afterwards to explain why it didn't happen.

I don't trust ex-President Clinton or her husband.

George Bush was frustrated with the negative spin the news reporters put into every story. At one point an aid remarked, "If he walked on water, the next day's headline would read "Bush Can't Swim."

Perhaps the reason that the laws of nature work so well is that there are no politicians involved.

One difference between death and taxes is that death doesn't get worse every time Congress meets.

Voting is how we tell some politicians who are running to go take a walk.

No wonder the circus is struggling to survive. All the clowns are in Washington D.C.

April 15th is when the government transfers the hole in its pocket to yours.

To bad the only people who know how to run the country are busy driving cabs and cutting hair.

The most perfect government is that under which a wrong to the humblest is an affront to all.

If absence makes the heart grow fonder, a lot of congressmen must really love their jobs.

What any political party really means when it calls for government reform:

Throw the rascals out and put our rascals in.

If you fool folks to get their money, it's fraud; if you fool them to get their vote, that's politics.

If you want to find out what's wrong with a man, elect him to public office.

Most problems are all in your mind. Unfortunately, paying taxes isn't one of them.

Diplomacy is the art of letting some one else have your way.

Only our individual faith in freedom can keep us free.

He who lives by the sword, dies by the sword.

With no vision, a nation will perish.

The New York Times is read by the people who run the country. The Washington Post is read by the people who think they run the country. The National Enquirer is read by people who believe Elvis is alive and running the country.

In statesmanship get the formalities right, never mind about the moralities.

The very ink with which all history is written is merely fluid prejudice.

There isn't a Parallel of Latitude but thinks it would have been the Equator if it had its rights.

Prosperity is the best protector of principle.

Politics is a profession where great skill is required, especially in making excuses.

Twelve Americans out of a quarter of a billion said O.J. was originally not guilty. You call that justice? – This time it was.

A trial isn't about truth, it's where twelve people vote for who constructs the best story.

Where law ends, tyranny begins.

It could probably be shown by fact and figures that there is no distinctly Native American criminal class except Congress.

It is by the goodness of God that in our country we have those three unspeakable precious things: Freedom of speech, freedom of conscience, and the prudence never to practice either of them.

The old ideas are new again because they are not old - duty, sacrifice, commitment, and a patriotism that finds expression in taking part and pitching in.

The only way to regenerate the world is to do the duty which lies nearest us.

Everybody should pay their taxes with a smile. I tried, but they wanted cash.

Americans are go-getters. Trouble is - we go get from Japan, China, and Europe.

The worst thing about political jokes is that some of them get elected.

Next time you think people have lost faith in America, consider how many are still signing up for 30-year mortgages.

Senator to newspaper reporter: "I spent $3 million to get elected to a $134,OOO-a-year job, and you expect me to balance the budget?"

Americans can handle any problem and we have the warning labels and recalls to prove it.

Opinion polls: A great way to find out what people are undecided about.

I can remember way back when a liberal was one who was generous with his own money.

The average politician wouldn't have to spend so much time mending fences if he did less sitting on them.

George Washington was the only President who didn't blame the previous administration for all his troubles.

Politics

April 15 is when you- realize the American Eagle does not get along on chicken feed.

After we grow up, we stop believing in fairy tales, except those told by politicians.

If the Ten Commandments were to be published today, the chances are they would be challenged immediately as discriminating against sinners.

The Lord giveth and the Lord taketh away; the government reverses the process.

Listening to a political speech is like archery: you must always make allowance for the wind.

If in 2008 your cup runneth over, the IRS will be right there in 2009 with a sponge.

A politician is someone who shows you a mirage in the desert and then tries to sell you a drinking cup.

I'm sure the people who established free speech didn't realize what people were going to be saying.

Take sides. Neutrality helps the oppressor, never the victim. Silence encourages the tormentor, never the tormented.

The government says it's going to step in unless the airlines do something about all the delayed flights, which sounds pretty good until you remember who's responsible for the post office.

In times of calamity any rumor is believed.

A government subsidy is like having your kid buy you an expensive gift on your credit card.

How about Hillary Clinton for President, and Bill for vice?

In America, everybody has a right to express an opinion, but fortunately nobody is compelled to listen.

If you want to kill an enemy, love him to death.

The way things are going, America's best hope this year is that we hold an election, and nobody wins.

The biggest cause of crooked politics is people who don't vote because of crooked politics.

The impersonal hand of government can never replace the helping hand of a neighbor.

When someone in government is said to have a natural bent for politics, that may just be a polite way of saying he's crooked.

Congress has made thousands of laws, but has never improved on the Ten Commandments.

For many today, freedom means the chance to crack down on some other guy's obnoxious habits. Oppression means having someone crack down on your obnoxious habits.

A political race is nothing but a hop, skip and jump affair - hop on the bandwagon, skip the facts, and jump on the opposition.

I.R.S. agent: We're rather proud of that jar, it's blood from a turnip.

Think of government regulations as a bottle of ketchup. You either get none, or a lot more than you want.

I'm from the government - I am here to help you.

Justice is a hope, not a certainty.

A lawsuit is a machine you enter as a pig and come out a sausage.

Let's not be too critical of the tobacco industry. After all, it has found a cure for old age.

A politician is a person who divides his time between running for office and running for cover.

Our government shut down because it has no budget and no money. Funny that never stopped any of us.

Ninety percent of politics is deciding whom to blame.

The politician's speech had the audience in the aisles - they were running for the exits.

Constant success shows us but one side of the world. For as it surrounds us with friends who will tell us only our merits, so it silences those enemies from whom alone we can learn our defects.

Politics

The City of Happiness is located in the State of Mind.

Freedom is not the right to do as you please, but the liberty to do as you ought.

A taxpayer is someone who's always feeding the hand that bites him.

Diplomacy is the wit of tipping your hat without tipping your hand.

If you think government isn't in the bedroom yet, just read the tag on your mattress.

I know nothing about computers, but the thing that has me worried sick is what do they know about me?

History repeats itself, but the script is always rewritten.

Americans will pay a big price for any invention that will help them to save time they won't know what to do with.

No computer can come up with a document as great as the declaration of independence - and that was written with a quill pen.

Wealth

Wealth

The only true wealth is self worth.

To think only of the pot of gold at the end of a rainbow is to miss the beauty of the rainbow itself.

Money still talks, but is has to catch it's breath a little more often now.

The only think harder to keep than a secret, is your money.

Money will buy all the friends in the world, but they are seldom worth the price.

He who imparts cheerfulness is adding to the wealth of the world.

When wealth is lost, nothing is lost; when health is lost, something is lost; when character is lost, all is lost.

It is easy to get everything you want, provided you first learn to do without the things you can not get.

Why is there so much month left at the end of the money.

If you want to feel rich, just count all of the things you have that money can't buy.

We should make a practice of spending our fund of criticism frugally and our fund of praise extravagantly.

To avoid a sudden shock, open your electricity bill slowly.

Great endowments to colleges are beautiful, but when a one-year-old gives part of his candy bar to a friend, that's philanthropy.

A dollar doesn't go far these days, but it doesn't stay around long either.

To a serious shopper, it's not how much an item costs; it's how you save that counts.

Debt is the devil in disguise.

There are plenty of 5 cent cigars still around, the trouble is they cost a quarter now.

There is always too much month left at the end of the money.

When a person with experience meets a person with money, the person with experience will get the money and the person with the money will get some experience.

Don't miss the beautiful colors of the rainbow while you're looking for the pot of gold at the end of it.

Financially, most of us are probably in the middle income and upper outgo bracket.

Fidelity bought with money can be overcome with money.

Isn't it strange how many people who have no problem giving the Lord credit are reluctant to give Him cash?

Money can't buy happiness but it makes shopping more fun.

The poor person is not one who is without a cent, but one who is without a dream.

Many receive advice - only the wise profit by it.

We really do not control memory. We just like or dislike what it decides to offer us.

There's no telling about investment advisers. One man's prophet is another man's loss.

A fool and his money never appear when you heed a loan.

When we have provided against cold, hunger and thirst, all the rest is but vanity and excess.

The cost of living is so high because yesterday's luxuries are always becoming today's necessities.

Some people dream of being something, others stay awake and are.

If you go through life spending like you have money to burn, you'll eventually find yourself sifting through the ashes.

A vacation is a holiday from everything but expenses.

Donald Trump reports the he actually does have a dime for every time he's been called a ruthless bloodsucker.

Wealth

Not long ago, you couldn't wait to get the salary you can't live on today.

More good has been accomplished by simple people seeking their own honest ends than by all the philanthropists in history.

If it's such a small world, why are phone bills so high?

Everyone likes something for nothing; even a millionaire likes a free pass to a ball game.

Remember when charity began at home and not in the tax accountant's office.

It's easy to make a buck. It's a lot tougher to make a difference.

An economist is someone who tries to save you money you don't have so you can spend it on something you don't need to support a government you don't want.

Money will buy a pretty good dog, but it won't buy the wag of his tail.

The manner in which it is given is worth more than the gift.

We all want the government to cut down on its spending, unless, of course, it affects us.

Collection agencies don't believe in putting off until tomorrow what can be dunned today.

Incomes are becoming biodegradable - they can disappear without a trace better than almost anything else.

Always remember, money isn't everything, but also remember to make a lot of it before talking such fool nonsense.

Fun is like life insurance: The older you get, the more it costs.

Mixed emotions is the feeling you get when you have just one payment left on your car, and you trade it in on another.

The law belongs to those who can buy it.

We're living in the plastic card age allowing us to spend our money before finding out there isn't any.

He who multiplies riches multiplies cares.

It's good to have money to buy things that money can buy, but it's better not to lose things that money cannot.

If the best things in life are free, why are the next best things so expensive?

Today's buying policy in brief: Purchase now, afford later.

Wealth is always a relative matter. The more wealth you have, the more relatives you hear from.

About the only thing you can do on a shoestring these days is trip.

The foremost status symbol used to be the car. Now it's being able to afford the repair bills.

Remember back when we saved money by saving it, rather than by buying things at some percent off?

Experience may not be worth what it costs, but we can't seem to get it for any less.

The popularity of professional sports is understandable. Where else could you watch a bunch of millionaires beat up on each other.

By the time some men have money to burn - the pilot light has gone out.

Money's a lot tighter since my second divorce. I just live from pay-chick to pay-chick.

Honor is purchased by the deeds we do.

A note from your credit card bank says, "Leave home without it."

A man should always consider how much he has more than he wants, and how much more unhappy he might be than he really is.

Misers may not be fun to live with, but they make wonderful ancestors.

The trouble with a fixed income is that there's no such thing as a fixed outgo.

Living on a budget is the same as living beyond your means except you have a record of it.

True wealth should not be calculated by money. It should he calculated by the number of beautiful memories a person has accumulated.

Wealth

Raising a family is more satisfying than getting rich because eventually you reach a point when you're willing to admit that you have enough.

Have you ever wondered why it's called "instant credit" when what it really means is "instant debt"?

Nothing improves self-worth like making a daily investment in kindness.

Money talks, the problem is, it is always saying goodbye.

If you think the youngsters of today do not know the value of money, try giving them a nickel.

Two can live as cheaply as one if both have bad taste.

Not too long ago a dime was a kid's weekly allowance. Now it's used as an emergency screwdriver.

The cost of living may be high, but the cost of dying is even worse.

Card playing can be expensive, but so can any game where you begin by holding hands.

Whoever says what goes up must come down isn't considering the cost of living.

A full-service broker can assist you in obtaining a loan and in finding a second job to pay for it.

The poor feel that their many problems would be magically solved if only they had more money. The rich feel that way too.

We can be generous and yet not spend money. Just give a pleasant word to a discouraged person.

Living from payday to payday used to be considered a disgrace. Now it is an accomplishment.

Money can't buy happiness, but it lets you get a bigger shopping bag.

Many an optimist has become rich by buying out a pessimist.

We have found wealth when we have found enjoyment in unbought pleasures.

By the time you finish paying for a house in the country, it's no longer the country.

Most of us consider budgeting to be a fate worse than debt.

The only things that are guaranteed to last a lifetime these days are the payments.

Most people don't really want to make money; they just want to collect it.

Most people would be satisfied with the money they have, if somebody else didn't have more.

Don't knock the rich. When was the last time you were hired by someone poor?

Every great fortune can be traced back to someone who was first to see the obvious.

There are three ways to lose in the stock market: getting in, staying in, and getting out.

We're better at deciding what we would do with a million dollars than what we're going to do without it.

If you want to feel rich just count the things money can't buy.

We, as a country, have always owed a great debt to our forefathers. Now we owe a great debt to everybody.

Wealthy people miss one of life's great thrills; making the last payment on an installment loan.

Goodness is the only investment that never fails.

The secret of managing money is to live as economically as the day after payday as you did the day before.

Beware of little expenses; a small leak will sink a great battleship.

There's a severe punishment for those people who live beyond their means - the debt penalty.

Borrow money from pessimists - they don't expect it back.

Luxuries, like children's toys, are a lot more fun if there aren't too many of them.

Judge a man's character not by what he drives, but by what drives him.

Wealth

Riches adorn the dwelling; virtue adorns the person.

I am so broke I can't even pay attention.

Proverb for installment buyers - all's well that ends.

No man is rich enough to buy back his past.

Ten cents used to be a lot of money for a kid, but dimes have changed.

Two wrongs don't make a right, but they could make two lawyers rich.

A true realty bargain is when you get good neighbors.

Joy is not what we own - it is in what we are.

Making money fast is not easier than making it first.

Despite inflation, a penny for some people's thoughts is still a fair price.

As you give, you gain, not necessarily monetarily, but in all of the more precious blessings of life.

Sharing what you have is more important than what you have.

If you wish to be remembered, leave a lot of debts.

Behind every great fortune is a crime.

Dimes don't buy much these days, but they still make excellent screwdrivers.

Riches adorn the dwelling - Virtue adorns the person.

It's not easy to hold what you don't have in your hands.

Make your heads save your heels.

Willful waste is woeful want.

Save your pennies, and the dollars will take care of themselves.

A penny saved is a penny earned.

Waste not, want not.

A wasteful woman can throw more food out with a spoon than her man can carry in with a shovel.

I can do without anything until I can pay for it.

Gather up the fragments that nothing be lost.

If you have money in your pocket, and you owe someone else money, you are carrying his money in your pocket.

Riches of life multiply when we share them with others

No matter what happens, it will make some attorney very wealthy.

There occasions when it is undoubtedly better to incur loss than to make gain.

The secret of thrift is to live as economically the day after payday as you do the day before.

There are two times in a man's life when he should not speculate; when he can't afford it and when he can.

Few of us can stand prosperity. Another man's I mean.

There's an old-time toast which is golden for its beauty. "When you ascend the hill of prosperity may you not meet a friend."

A fool and his money are soon parted, but a fool and his credit cards are always together.

Money is a cruel master, but a kind servant.

The best way to improve the value of your car is to trade it in and then try to buy it back.

Remember that even a bargain costs money.

It's not what we have, but how we take care of what we have that counts.

The old cow will want her tail at fly time.

A fool and his money is soon parted.

Prices haven't gone up on everything, for example, problems are still a dime a dozen.

Wealth

Most men and women have to have get-up-and-go so their savings won't.

The first thing you should pack for two weeks of vacation is four weeks of money.

A good salesman is one who can convince his wife that she looks too fat in a mink coat.

The new 'Divorced Barbie' comes with all of Ken's worldly things.

It is better to give than to lend, and it costs about the same.

Often the worst thing to give someone is pity.

ATTORNEY: "I believe a man is innocent until he runs out of money."

Speaking of nostalgia, remember when things were priced "AT" instead of "FROM".

Your gifts have little value if your heart isn't wrapped up in them.

Learning to enjoy inexpensive things can be just as gratifying as being rich.

If money talks, mine must have laryngitis.

Contentment comes not from greater wealth, but from fewer wants.

A budget helps you pay as you go if you don't go any place.

Inflation marches on, making it possible for people in all walks of life to live in more expensive neighborhoods without even moving.

It's amazing how generous many people think they are because they give free advice.

When people talk about "spending" your vacation, they really know what they're talking about.

Money may not be everything, but it is handy till you get everything.

If you've got it, flaunt it, and watch how many people you turn off.

The only thing that goes faster than a new car is the time between payments.

Money can't buy happiness, but it's a good bargaining chip.

If you think the art of conversation is dead, try hiring two carpenters by the hour.

The person who agrees with everything you say either isn't paying attention or else plans to sell you something.

Life is just an eternal struggle to keep one's earning capacity up to one's yearning capacity.

No after-dinner speaker is more appreciated than the one who is quick to say, "I'll take the check."

Money can be lost in more ways than won.

While we are trying to keep up with the family next door, they are probably trying to keep up with us.

The cost of living is always the same - all you have.

If you want to give something to a person who already has everything, give him sympathy.

I have the greatest of all riches, that of not desiring them.

Considering that crime does not pay, it's amazing how many people are willing to work at it.

Money can't buy friends, but it can rent them for a while.

He: "But, darling, you said there was something about me that you could love."
She: "Yeah, but you spent it all."

Despite all the complaints about the high cost of living, most of us still think it's worth it.

The nice thing about giving money as a gift is one size fits all.

One day while in a card store, I couldn't help but notice their sign. It read: Prices on everything are going up, but our writing paper remains stationery.

I made a killing in the market. I shot my broker.

Wealth

One advantage of being poor is that it puts a limit on the kind of sinning you can afford.

Nothing depreciates a car more than an attempt to trade it in.

Poverty has another advantage - it helps you find out what you can do without.

Think positive! The less money you have, the more there is to get.

There is a difference between folks who love money and folks who love money and are willing to work hard for it.

I have a balanced monthly budget. I worry as much about the money I don't have as I do about the money I do have.

The more a person loves money, the more expensive things become.

Remember that the person who steals an egg will steal a chicken.

When you're uncertain of what you should pay someone, ask, "What do you think is fair?" You'll almost always get a reasonable answer.

Many people claim that money is the root of all evil, but very few of them try to be good by giving it all away.

A fool and his money are invited places.

A bargain is something we buy, but can't explain why.

It's true money can't buy happiness, but it can make unhappiness a lot nicer.

All Creatures Great and Small

All Creatures Great and Small

You can judge how civilized a man is by the degree of compassion he exhibits for lesser creatures.

If you can't teach an old dog new tricks, get a new dog.

Animals are not as dumb as people think. Have you ever seen one jogging five miles before breakfast?

A duck's quack doesn't echo and no one knows why.

Elephants are the only animals that can't jump.

Never try to teach a pig to sing; it wastes your time, and it annoys the pig.

If it looks like a duck, walks like a duck, and quacks like a duck, cook it.

If you think you're too small to make a difference, you haven't been in bed with a mosquito.

The real reason a dog is man's best friend is that it doesn't understand a word you are saying.

A bone to the dog is not charity - Charity is the bone shared with the dog when you are just as hungry as the dog.

Never approach a bull from the front, a horse from the rear, or a fool from any direction.

Why are birds grouch in the morning? Because their bills are over dew.

Would a fly without wings be called a walk?

Turtles theory — nothing happens until you stick your neck out.

Puppies still have bad breath even after eating a tic-tac.

Did you hear about the two male silkworms that raced for the love of a female silkworm and ended up in a tie?

Some men learn about forgiveness by studying the lives of saints, and some of us keep dogs.

Even a mosquito doesn't get a slap on the back until it starts to work.

Every dog has his day.

A lawsuit is a machine you enter as a pig and come out as a sausage.

If you can't run with the big dogs, stay on the porch.

Turtle soup is never served in a fast food restaurant.

If a creature as smart and as strong as an elephant can work for peanuts, why should you object?

There was a time when people spoke of a workhorse and it was a horse.

Never buy a dog at a flea market.

I think men, women, and animals make equally good friends.

Horsepower was much safer when only horses had it.

Contrary to what most think, dogs do talk. They speak the language of love.

I feel sorry for Princess Di. How could she have known she kissed the wrong frog?

Our minds are like old horses; we must exercise them if we wish to keep them in working order.

When you see a turtle on top of a fence, you know someone gave him a lift.

I wish I were as wonderful as my dog thinks I am.

If you hoot with the owls at night, you can't soar with the eagles in the morning.

My dog is not spoiled - I'm just well trained.

Beware the dog that comes bringing a bone, for he will carry another when he goes home.

When the cat's away, the mice will play.

A dog never shows bigotry in selecting a master.

Don't kill the goose that lays the golden egg.

Sin is a silent dog that finally bites its master.

All Creatures

I have a horse that walks normally sometimes, and sometimes he limps.
What should I do?
The next time he walks normally, try to sell him.

I thought it was cats that had nine lives, not leftovers.

Call to veterinarian - "We can't get our new bulldog to open his mouth,
and there's a burglar in it."

A dog is born with the need to love and never outgrows it.

Money will buy you a fine dog, but only kindness will make him wag his
tail.

Man is the only animal that can be skinned more than once.

GIRL: How much are your puppies?
BOY: They are all 75 cents except the black one, he is 85 cents.
GIRL: Why is he 85 cents?
BOY: He swallowed a dime yesterday.

Teenagers are the only known mammals that wake up asleep.

It's difficult to be angry at a puppy wagging its tail.

Dictionary

211

Dictionary

You can't find the meaning of life in the dictionary.

The dictionary is the only place where success comes before work.

Adolescence	An embarrassing time of life when everyone's parents turn stupid simultaneously.
Age	A high price to pay for maturity.
Bachelor	A man who never Mrs. anything.
Bachelor	A rolling stone that has gathered no boss.
Bachelor	Someone who opposes marriage, because it means being put on a wife support system.
Bank	An institution where you can borrow money if you can present sufficient evidence that you don't need it.
Bargain	Something that you can't use at a price you can't resist.
Belly Dancing	Navel maneuvers.
Bore	Someone who spawns yawns.
Born Loser	Someone who gets a paper cut from a get well card.
Bresaurant	A restaurant such as Hooters.
Budget	Valuable tool that supplies you with oversight, insight and hindsight, as well as a perfect excuse for you to say later "See, I really did try."
Busy Body	It's better than a busybody.
Busybodies	People who can't leave bad enough alone.

Capital Punishment	What we get when congress is in session.
Car Sickness	The feeling that you get every month when the payment comes due.
Career Woman	One who prefers to go out and be an employee rather than stay home and be boss.
Cash	A four-letter word for dad.
Character	A jerk with personality.
Christmas	The season when a smart child writes a letter to Santa Claus, but a smarter one writes to Grandma.
Classic	A book which people praise and don't read.
Cleaning ladies	People who take a bite out-of a grime.
Committee	A group of the unwilling, picked from the unfit to do the unnecessary.
Committee	A group of people who talk for hours to produce something known as minutes.
Compulsive Shopping	A buy-illogical urge.
Conceit	God's gift to little men.
Conscience	The I witness who knows all about me.
Conscience	The thing that makes you feel awful when everything else feels wonderful.
Credit	The system that allows you to live the way you would if you could.
Depression	A time when you have no belt to tighten.

Dictionary

Detective Agency	Snooper market.
Diet	A meal with all the slimmings.
Diet Willpower	Feast fight.
Divorce	Where 'I do' becomes 'adieu'
Dual Air Bags	A political debate.
Economist	An expert who will know tomorrow why the things he predicted yesterday didn't happen.
Economist	Someone who thinks he knows more about money than the people who have it.
Education	What you get when reading the small print.
Emergency Room	A place where your symptoms are diagnosed after a thorough examination of your assets.
Engagement	A period of urge on the verge of a merge.
Eraser	A corrector's item.
Etiquette	Learning to yawn with your mouth closed.
Extravagance	How other people spend their money.
Failure	The fertilizer of success.
Fatness	The past tense of fitness.
Flood	A river that's become too big for its bridges.
Frenzied Secretary	Hyper typer.

Genius	A crackpot whose goofy idea makes millions.
Goals	Dreams with deadlines.
Gossip	One who does his work with pry and joy.
Greedy Person	Someone who grabs more than you can grab.
Grouch	One who goes by rule of glum.
Hangover	Something to occupy a head that wasn't used the night before.
Hypochondriac	Person who, when the doctor assures him he's in perfect health, asks for a second opinion.
Hypochondriac	One whose claims to being an invalid are invalid.
Insurance Adjuster	Expert who knows exactly which clause excludes the accident you just had.
Intellectual	Someone who can bore you and make you feel guilty about it.
Jogging Buff	Lope addict.
Lawyer	Someone who is willing to go out and spend your last cent to prove that he is right.
Lawyer's Apartment	Legal pad.
Librarian	Someone who does have all the answers.
Luck	Often nothing, but a tricky name for hard work.
Man	A creature made at the end of a week's work when God was tired.
Marriage	A solid that dissolves if it cools.

Marriage	An institution held together by three books - Good, Cook, and check.
Medical Specialist	A doctor who charges you a lot for seeing you a little.
Memoir	Book that proves that confession is good for the sale.
Middle Age	When anything new in life is likely to be a symptom.
Middle Age	When a man returns a wink with a blink.
Middle Age	When you still have a lot on the ball, but you are to tired to bounce it.
Miser	One who is generous to a vault.
Modesty	A triumph of mind over flatter.
Monastery	Home for unwed fathers.
Music Lover	One who knows how to play the bagpipes, but chooses not to.
Nostalgia	Life in the past lane.
Nostalgia	A memory that cuts us down to sighs.
Nostalgia	Recalling things we never noticed when they happened.
Obituary Notice	The Mourning news.
Old Age	A time when actions creak louder than words.
Old Timer	One who remembers when time was marching on, not running out.
Opportunist	Any person who goes ahead and does what you always intended to do.
Optimist	Are wrong just as often as pessimists, but they have a lot more fun.

Optimist	Someone who sticks a stamp on the envelope before addressing it.
Panic	A time when you have no pants to bold up.
Pessimist	A person who is seasick during the entire voyage of life.
Pessimist	One who complains about the noise when opportunity knocks.
Politician	A person who is sworn in and cursed out.
Politician	Someone who thinks twice before saying nothing.
Politician	Someone who approaches every subject with an open mouth.
Procrastination	The condition that comes to those who have so much to do it drives them lazy.
Rare Book	One that comes back after you've loaned it.
Recession	A time when we tighten our belts.
Reliable Source	The one who started the rumor.
Retirement	That time of life when one no longer gets paid for loafing.
Rules of the Road	Something that some people make up as they go along.
Sandwich Spread	What people get when they snack too much between meals.
Self Confidence	Self-confidence is the ability to endure misfortune without looking for someone to blame.
Smirk	A pleasant, friendly smile on the face of somebody you don't like.

Dictionary

Smog	Air apparent.
Socialized Medicine	When women get together at a card party to talk about their operations.
Special Delivery	Every baby's birth.
Speed Limit	What a person follows as soon as he sees a police car.
Spendthrift	Someone who thinks a nest egg is for the birds.
Statesman	A politician who already has all the money he needs.
Summertime	When children slam the doors they left open all winter.
Sunbathing	A fry in the ointment.
Tact	Ability to tell a man he's open-minded when he has a hole in his head.
Tact	The ability to keep your shirt on while getting something off your chest.
Tax Collector	A civil servant who tends toward the lien and mean.
Tax Reform	Something that always benefits someone else.
Taxes	Five letter word that generates four-letter words.
Taxpayer	Another name for a political prisoner.
Travel Brochure Writer	A person who has away with words.
War	God's way of teaching us geography.

Wedding Chapel	Nave of hearts.
Will	A dead giveaway.
Willpower	Ability to eat only one salted peanut.
Workaholic	A workaholic is someone whose favorite enter-tainment is Monday morning.
Worn-out Locksmith	Hasp been.
Worry	The interest paid by those who borrow trouble.
Yawn	Nature's way of letting a married man open his mouth.

Things to Live By

- Say 'please' a lot.
- Live beneath your means.
- Buy whatever kids are selling on card tables in their front yards.
- Treat everyone you meet as you want to be treated.
- Donate two pints of blood every year.
- Make new friends but cherish the old ones.
- Don't waste time learning the tricks of the trade. Instead learn the trade.
- Admit your mistakes.
- Be brave, even if you're not, pretend to be. No one can tell the difference.
- Choose a charity in your community and support it generously with your time and money.
- Read the Bill of Rights.
- Use credit cards only for convenience, never for credit.
- Give yourself a year and read the Bible cover to cover.
- Learn to listen. Opportunity sometimes knocks very softly.
- Never deprive someone of hope; it might he all he or she has.
- Pray not for things, but for wisdom and courage.
- Never take action when you're angry.
- Pave good pasture.
- Enter a room with purpose and confidence.
- Don't discuss -business in elevators. You never know who may overhear you.
- Never pay for work before it's completed.
- Be willing to lose a battle in order to win, the war.
- Beware of the person who has nothing to lose.
- Keep secrets.
- Never cheat.
- Don't gossip.
- Say 'Thank You' a lot.

Index

A

B

C

Index

222

Index

Index

Endnote

Don't cry because it's over, smile because it happened.

Everything is always OK in the end.

If it's not, then it's not the end.

Here is a test to see if your mission on earth is complete:

If you're alive, it isn't.